Cut-Out Models and Instructions Included

the JOY of Flying Paper Airplanes

By Tatsuo Yoshida

DAVID & CHARLES
Newton Abbot London

the JOY of Flying Paper Airplanes

By Tatsuo Yoshida

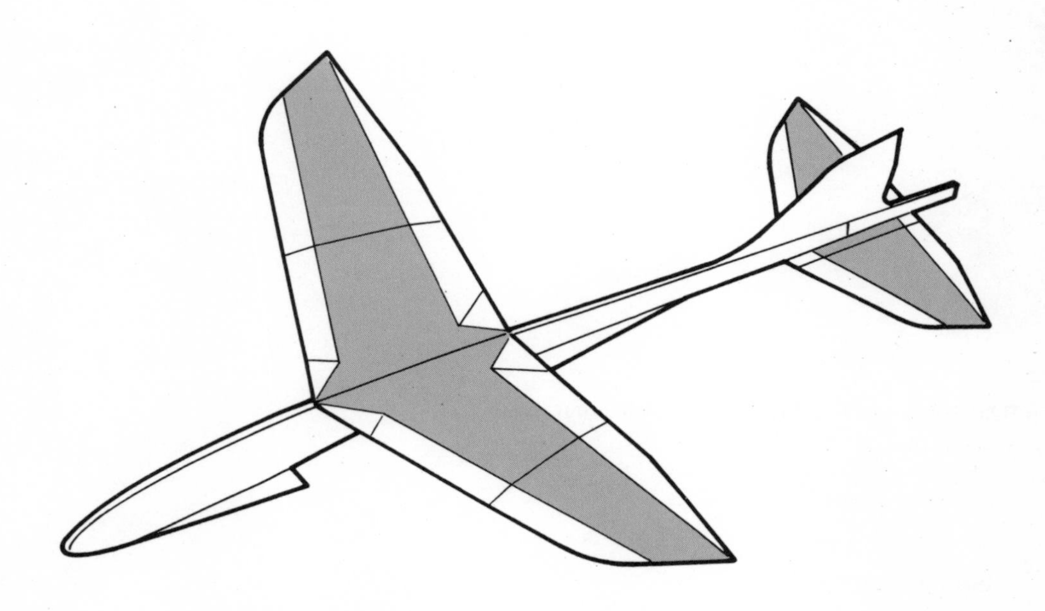

DAVID & CHARLES
Newton Abbot London

British Library Cataloguing-In-Publication data:

Yoshida, Tatsuo
The joy of flying paper airplanes.
1. Paper airplane.
I. Title.
745.592 TT174.5.P3

ISBN: 0-7153-9142-9

First published in Great Britain
by David & Charles 1988

Printed in Japan
for David & Charles Publishers plc
Brunel House
Newton Abbot Devon

TABLE OF CONTENTS

ASSEMBLY AND FLYING TECHNIQUES

MODELS

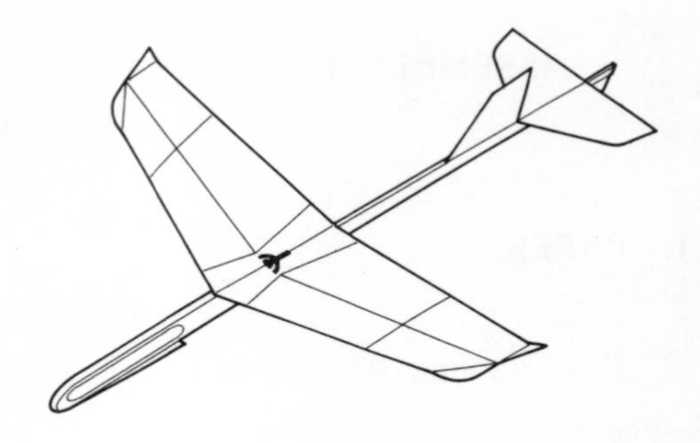

FOREWORD

The Second International Paper Airplane Convention was held on May 24, 1985 at the Kingdome Stadium in Seattle, Washington. There were 4,348 entries from 20 countries, and my models won both first and second place in the professional division for endurance and trick gliding. These victories meant the realization of my dream of winning, a dream I have had since the First International Paper Airplane Convention was held in 1967.

I have designed more than 140 paper airplanes, but for this book I have chosen those models that perform especially well and are interestingly styled. Paper airplanes are fun to make as well as to fly. This wonderful combination of hobby and sport can provide great enjoyment to people throughout the world.

It is often said that records are made to be broken. I hope that the paper airplanes in these pages provide you with stepping stones to your own creations and inspire you to become Number One.

May 1987
Tatsuo Yoshida

ASSEMBLY TECHNIQUES

1. PAPER

The paper in this book is made especially for paper airplanes. Should you need additional paper, use any similar paper (cover stock) available at stationery or art supply stores. 8½" x 11" size paper is the easiest to handle.

In designing, be sure to align the long wing and body with the grain of the paper, otherwise the paper airplane will easily break. Paper folds most easily and cleanly along the grain.

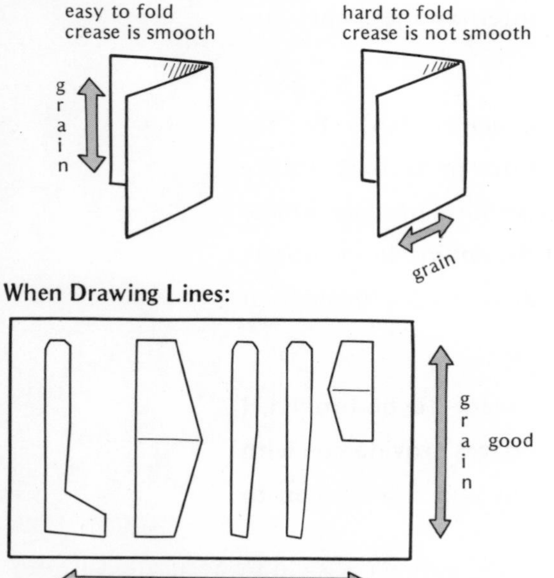

2. GLUE

Any type of glue, such as Elmer's transparent glue, is appropriate. Be sure to recap after each usage.

Simple models such as the "Little Sparrow" will not require glue. Transparent tape or staples should be sufficient.

3. TOOLS

a. **Scissors:** Preferably large.

b. **Exacto knife:** Use when there are many straight lines to cut. Remember to protect cutting surface with a mat or thick paper.

c. **Stylus:** An old ball point pen (without ink) or an ice pick may be used to create creases for fold lines.

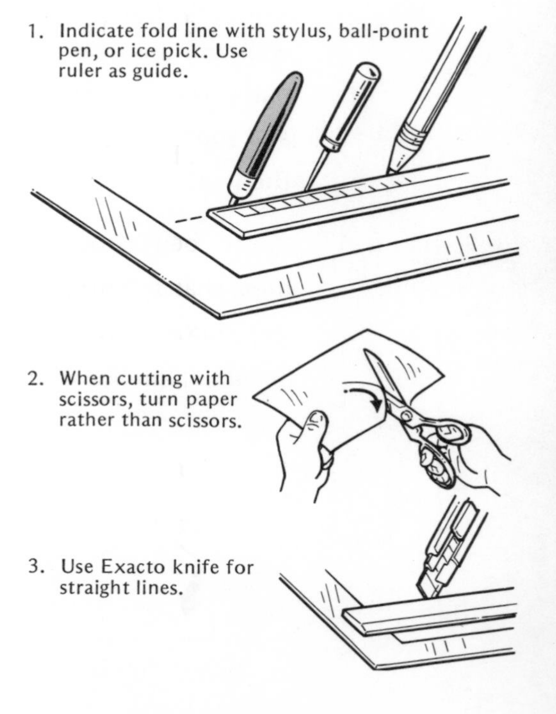

4. OTHER USEFUL TOOLS

a. **Spring clips of various sizes:** Use clips to hold glued sections together or for standing or suspending, as illustrated.

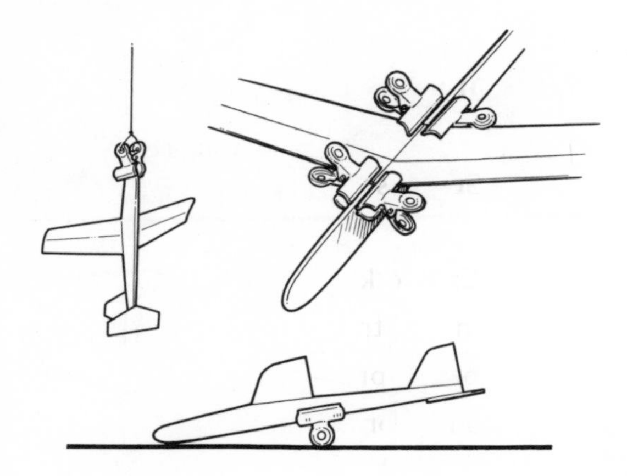

b. **Sandpaper:** Nos. 400 to 800 are most useful. No. 600 can be used for all sandpapering needs. Sand away sharp edges as well as excess glue that has dried and hardened.

5. TO REMOVE MODEL PAGE:

As in the illustration below, open the book as flat as possible and remove the entire page first with an Exacto knife.

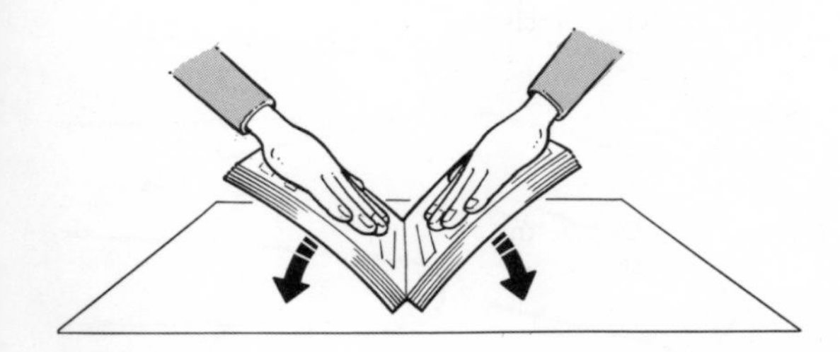

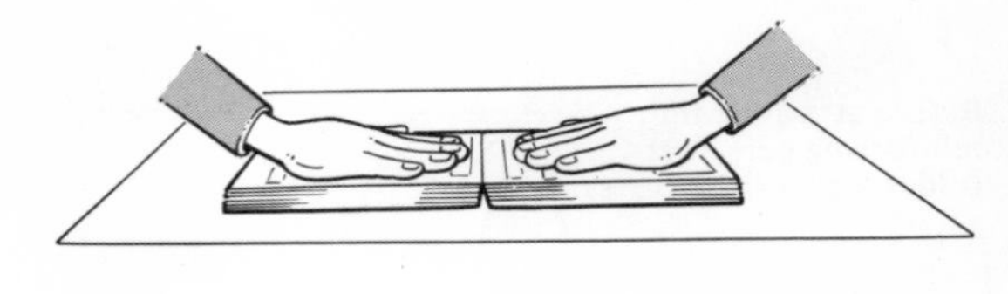

6. TO CUT MODEL:

Crease along cutting lines with stylus. Roughly cut out each model part, then cut each part again carefully, turning the paper rather than the scissors to cut curved areas. Do not cut fold lines or sections to be glued.

7. FOLDING

Use a ruler when folding. The center line of the wing, which attaches to the main body (fuselage), should first be folded at a 90° angle. Other parts should be folded to conform to the required angles. The dihedral angle should be accurate. Cut out gauges from the book to measure the accuracy of the angles.

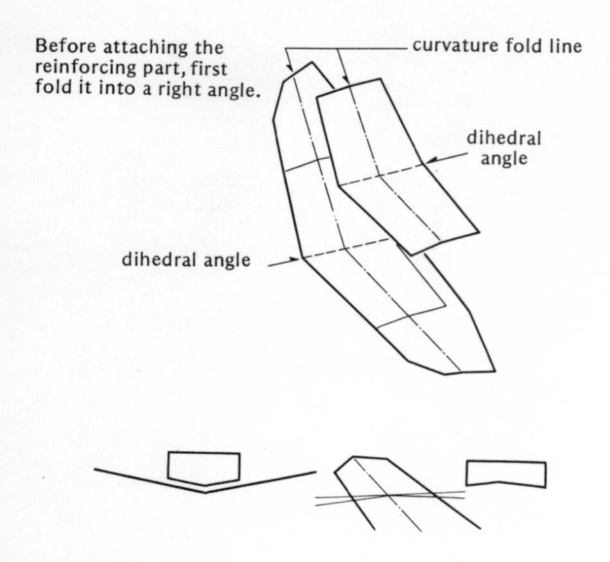

8. ASSEMBLY

First, assemble parts without glue. After verifying where all the parts go, apply glue to complete the model. Remember that the glue will dry quickly. Try to apply it evenly and to keep the parts straight. Pay special attention to attaching the wing to the fuselage section.

Use clips to hold the glued parts together until completely dry. Once the glue dries, adjustments are difficult. Before it dries, be sure that the wings are not crooked. Remove all excess glue.

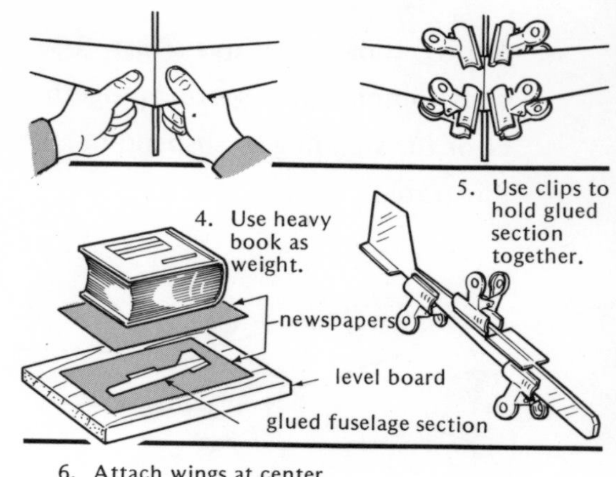

6. Attach wings at center.

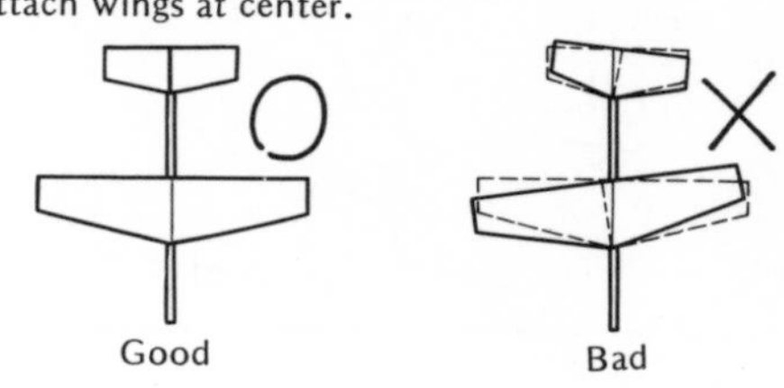

9. AFTER ASSEMBLY

The completed model should be suspended from a string or stood on a clip. Double-check all glued parts for errors. Polish the nose section with sand-paper and apply glue to strengthen the body.

Be sure the model is completely dry before flying it.

Sand Down and Glue

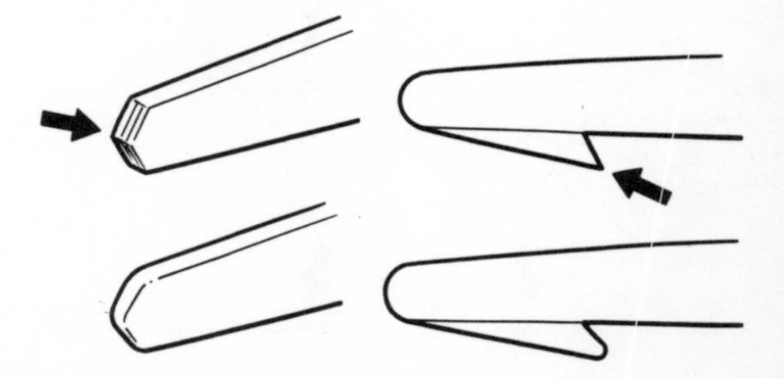

10. PAINTING

Enamel paint will strengthen the model. You may use clear lacquer as a base before painting.

HINTS FOR BETTER FLIGHT

1. THINGS TO CHECK:

a. Is the glue completely dry?

b. Are the parts glued together securely?

c. Are the fuselage and wings straight, not twisted?

d. Is the dihedral angle correct?

Check Before Flying

2. TEST FLIGHT AND ADJUSTMENT

The test flight should be held on a calm day.

Hold the model airplane at eye level and launch it slightly downward. Launch speed varies according to each model.

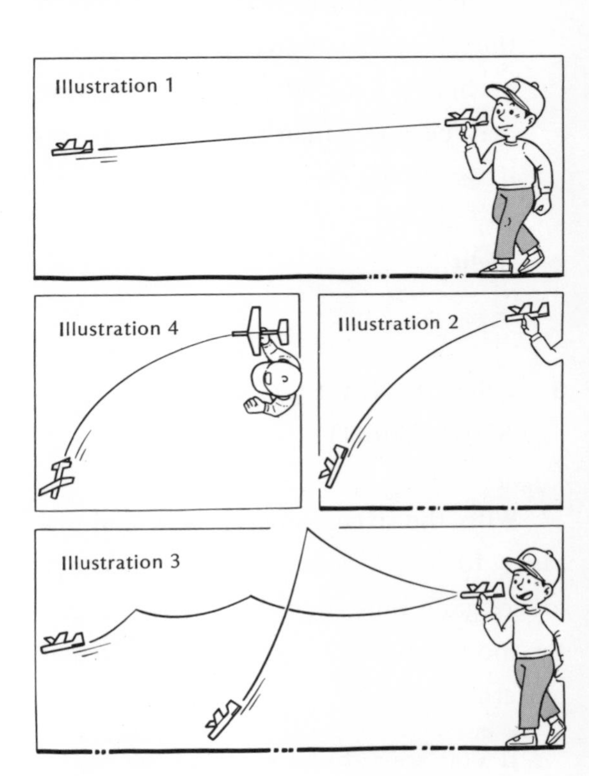

Illustration 1: This is a good flight pattern.

Illustration 2: You may be launching downward too much. Try pushing forward more when launching. If the airplane continues to fly downward, adjust the stabilizer by raising the elevators or bending the ailerons of the main wing slightly down.

Illustration 3: Both flight patterns may be due to either a weak launch or an upward launch. Try to achieve more speed when launching. If the model does not fly smoothly, turn elevators of stabilizer slightly downward.

Illustration 4: If the model veers to the left and nose-dives, the rudder may be bent to the left, or the right wing may be lower than the left. However, if the model veers to the left without any nosedive, it is ideal for endurance flight.

3. ENDURANCE FLYING AND ADJUSTMENTS

With the exceptions of trick and distance flights, a good flight consists of a longer glide time. In order to glide longer, the model must fly high and in a circular pattern.

If you are right-handed and the model flies straight ahead or to the right, adjust it to fly in a circular pattern to the left. The following adjustments may be necessary: bending the aileron area (back edge of main wing) of the right wing downward; bending the back of the rudder to the left; or slanting the stabilizer 3° to 5° to the right. Test-fly after each adjustment is made.

If the model somersaults as speed increases, adjust the elevator area (back edge of the stabilizer) by bending it slightly downward.

4. LAUNCHING BY HAND

Hold the fuselage under the wings, between thumb and index finger. (Index finger may be placed behind the wing; choose the style most comfortable for you.) Face into the wind and launch the airplane, tilting slightly to the right and upward. Practice increasing launch speed.

5. SLING LAUNCH

Use an 18" to 20" flat rubber band and tie one end to a stick. Launching by sling increases speed, so double-check the sturdiness of the model. Also, beware of hitting anyone.

For models ascending straight up (adjustment made on the stabilizer only), launch as horizontally as possible and point upward about 60°.

For gradually ascending models (adjustments made to wings and rudder), launch by tilting slightly to the right and pointing upward about 45°. Launching angle may be adjusted for each model.

Continual adjustment is necessary as you test-fly the model. The test-flying cycle should be repeated until the flight pattern is perfect.

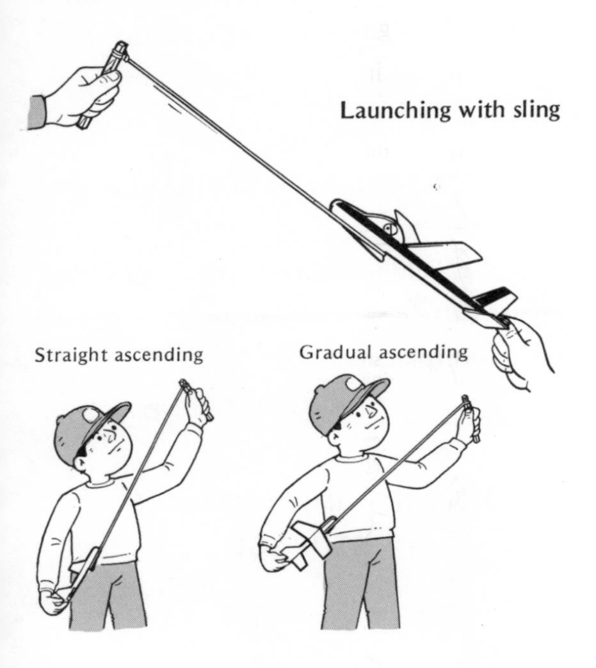

6. AIR CURRENTS

Outdoors, it is important for the airplane to catch an air current, for then it will glide effortlessly for a great distance. Contest winners are usually very skilled in catching air currents. Ascending air currents are created when warm air rises. This occurs on windless days and is very rare, so be patient. Air currents do not exist on windy days, thus you should wait for another day. A calm day on which you feel warm air on your cheeks is the sign of ascending air currents. This is the ideal time to fly your paper airplane.

ENJOYING YOUR PAPER AIRPLANE

The greatest joy comes from seeing your own creation fly high into the sky and disappear. Your regret in losing the airplane is overcome by your excitement. There is always the chance that you or someone else might find your airplane, so don't forget to put your name, address, and phone number on your models.

1. CONTESTS WITH FRIENDS

There are many ways to enjoy flying paper airplanes.

a. **Distance Contest:** The winner is the model that glides the farthest.

b. **Trick Contest:** Select judges. The model that flies in the most interesting pattern is the winner. Normally, paper airplanes can do somersaults, somersaults with half-turns, and descents in circular motions. Set up a hoop as in the following illustration, and try to get the model to somersault through it.

You can also set up a pole and have the airplane make U-turns around it.

c. **Landing Contest:** Create a miniature landing strip some distance from the starting line. Try to land your model on the landing strip. The winner is the model that is eliminated last.

Or, various prizes may be placed on the ground, with contestants trying to land their models directly on the prizes they desire.

Still another game might be to target a model to hit a bull's-eye.

d. **Relay Contest:** This is a team contest wherein one member launches from a starting line. After the model lands, a second team member then launches it from the landing site. Each team member takes turns flying the model until it goes around a course. The team that completes the course first is the winning team.

e. **Catching Contest:** This game calls for two persons to a team. They stand facing each other about 20' or 30' apart and fly airplanes to each other. The winning team is the one that catches the most models.

2. A CONTEST WITH YOURSELF

a. **Catching Contest:** After launching, attempt to catch your model airplane.

REPAIR – IMPROVEMENT – STORAGE

If the nose is damaged, scrape off the damaged area with a sharp Exacto knife, sand it down, and glue generously. Repairs, improvements, and painting will disturb the balance of the airplane, so you must add weight to balance it.

Transparent tape may be used to mend the wings, and another paper of similar weight may be glued onto the underwings, as illustrated in the following diagram. After the glue dries, cut off the excess paper along the wings.

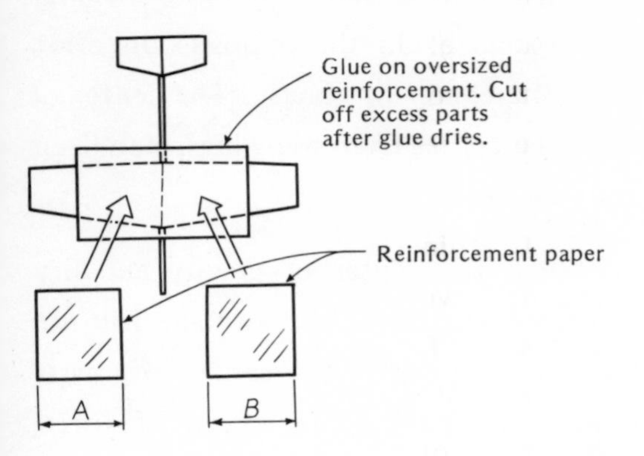

STORING YOUR AIRPLANES

The best way to store paper airplanes is to hang them on strings. Do not leave them leaning against the wing, for this will interfere with the balance of the dihedral angle.

For transporting, pack your model clamped to a box, as illustrated, so that it will not move around.

Carry model in box with spring clip.

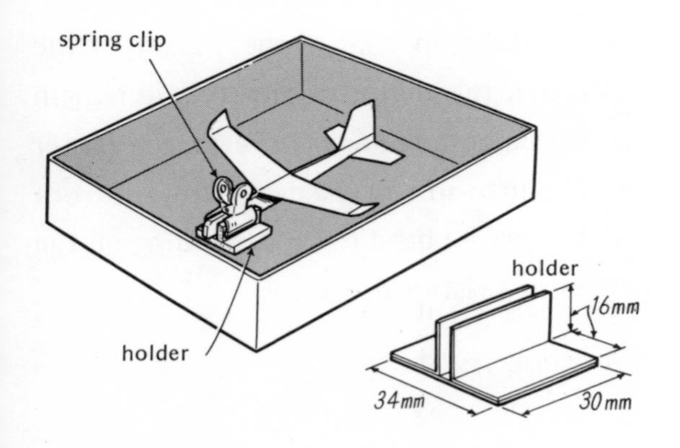

WHY DO AIRPLANES FLY?

Whether a jumbo jet or a small paper airplane, flying is the same. Both need wings and must move forward to fly. Forward motion is called "thrust." For paper airplanes, thrust is created by hand or a rubber band launching. Resistance, called "drift," is created by air to force the airplane backwards. Drift works on the wings and changes into a force called "lift," which pushes the airplane upward. The force called "gravity" pulls downward on the airplane.

When a paper airplane flies horizontally, it means that the lift and gravity are balanced. An increase in thrust means that the airplane will fly with more speed, resulting in more lift. Less speed means that lift is less than gravity, resulting in descending flight. Paper airplanes use the force of gravity and change it into thrust-force. This is like riding downhill on a bicycle without pedaling and is called "gliding."

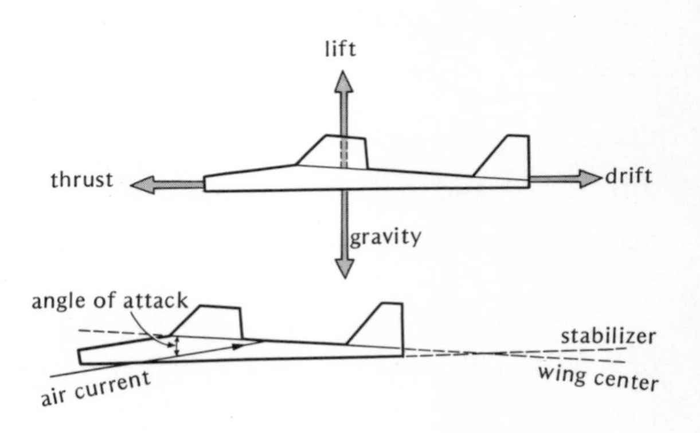

To change drift-force into lift-force, the wing must be angled slightly upward. This is called the "angle of attack." The angle of attack must be adjusted so that there is maximum lift-force and minimum drift-force.

The main wing alone cannot maintain balance constantly. It requires the stabilizer wing also. When the angle of attack on the wing is too great, drift rather than lift increases. The stabilizer wing helps to stabilize the airplane by automatically forcing a horizontal glide. This force is called "vertical stabilizing."

The main wing will always have curvature on the top side. This increases the force of lift.

If the airplane does not glide evenly, this means that the lift-force from both sides of the wings is unbalanced. The stabilizer prevents unbalancing of the lift-force and veering.

When the airplane tilts to either side, it must be able to return to the horizontal position. On paper airplanes, both wings are raised at the tips. This is called the dihedral angle, which stabilizes horizontal balance.

Now you can see that thrust, lift, directional and horizontal stabilizing are necessary for a paper airplane to fly.

Another important aspect is the center of gravity. This can be located by balancing the airplane on the tip of your finger.

When an airplane is flying, the center of lift-force is in the opposite direction from the center of gravity. The center of lift-force comes from the wings, stabilizer, and fuselage.

When the center of gravity and lift-force are separated, the airplane will not fly. For example, if the center of gravity is in front of the center of the lift-force, the nose becomes heavier and causes the airplane to nose-dive. To correct this, you must raise the back of the stabilizer (elevator area), which will move the lift-force toward the front, closer to the center of gravity. You may also move the center of gravity toward the rear by making the nose area lighter.

If the airplane does not fly because the nose section is too light, reverse the adjustment process.

Unlike the center of gravity, you cannot see the center of lift-force. However, a good flying airplane will have the two centers close to one another.

Unless you change the weight of the airplane, the center of gravity will remain in the same location. However, the center of the lift-force may change toward front and back, left and right, depending on the bend or twist of the wings.

ADJUSTMENTS FOR POOR FLIGHT PATTERNS

Following are possible reasons your paper airplane may not fly smoothly even though it is in perfect condition:

- Airplanes cannot fly well when wind is swirling around buildings or when rough air currents exist. Try flying your model where there is no wind.
- When launching by hand, the timing of your release may need adjustment.
- Your rubber band may be too weak or too strong.
- Check the dihedral angle.
- Check fuselage from front, side, and back for straight lines. It is easy to see if the main wings are twisted but difficult to find the backward bending of both wings.
- Check the stabilizer from all sides.
- The glue may not be applied evenly, resulting in throwing the center of gravity off balance. Adjust by adding weights or scraping off excess glue.
- There may be hollow areas created by insufficient glue. Paper airplane models are usually fragile and tend to go off balance easily. Apply glue to hollow sections with a toothpick or piece of paper.

FEATURES OF A PAPER AIRPLANE

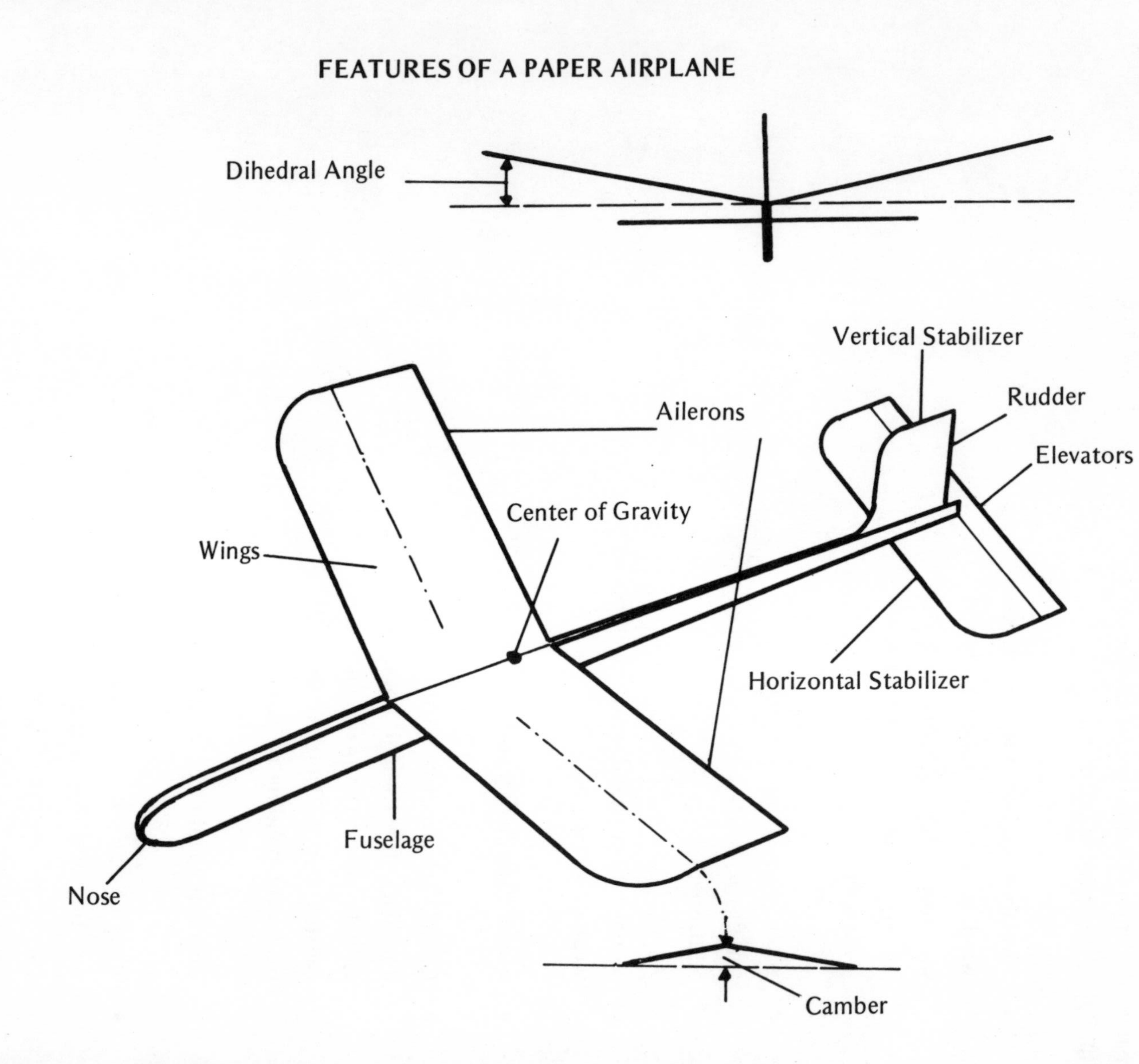

the JOY of Flying Paper Airplanes

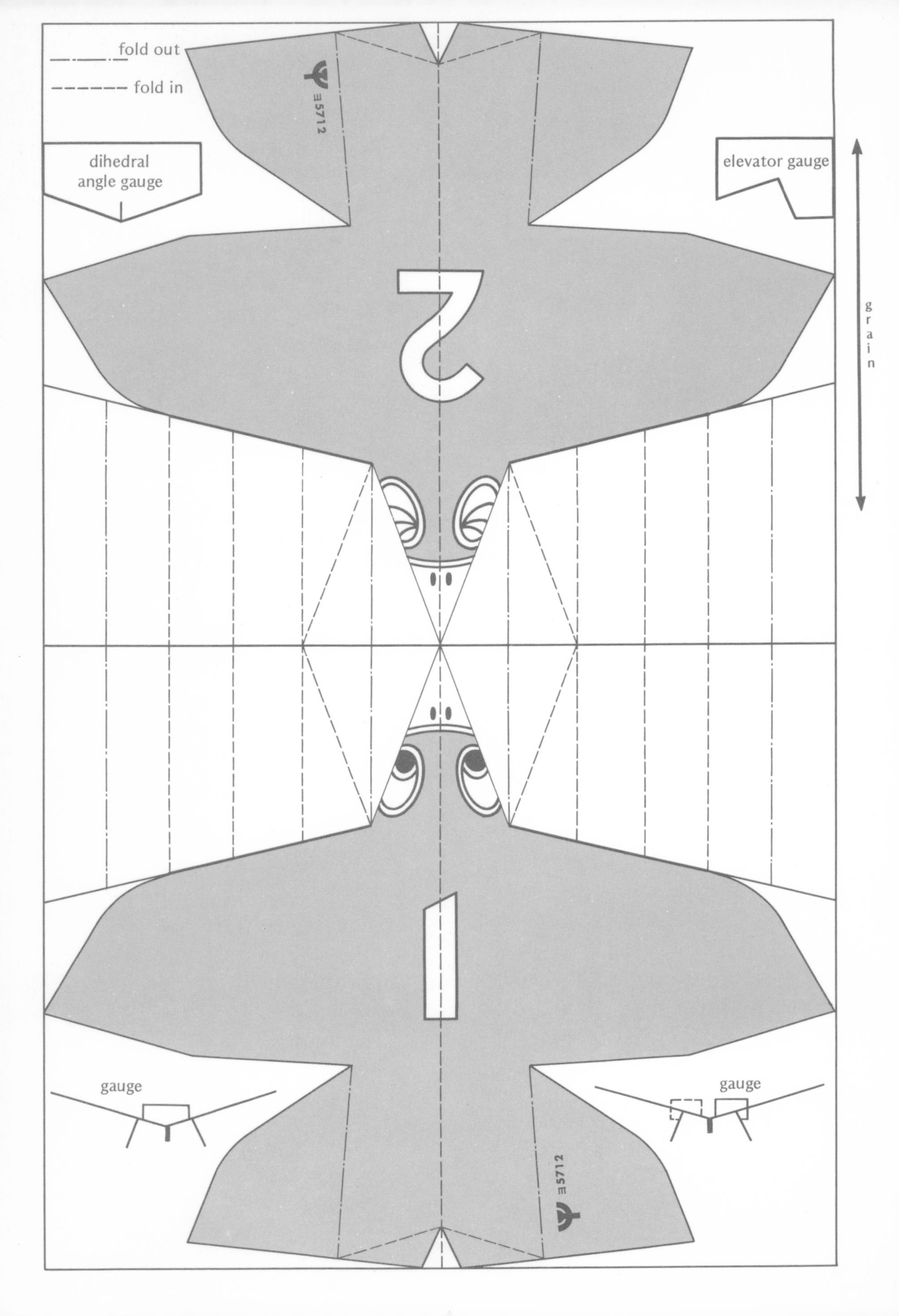
fold out
fold in
dihedral angle gauge
elevator gauge
grain
2
1
gauge
gauge
5712
5712

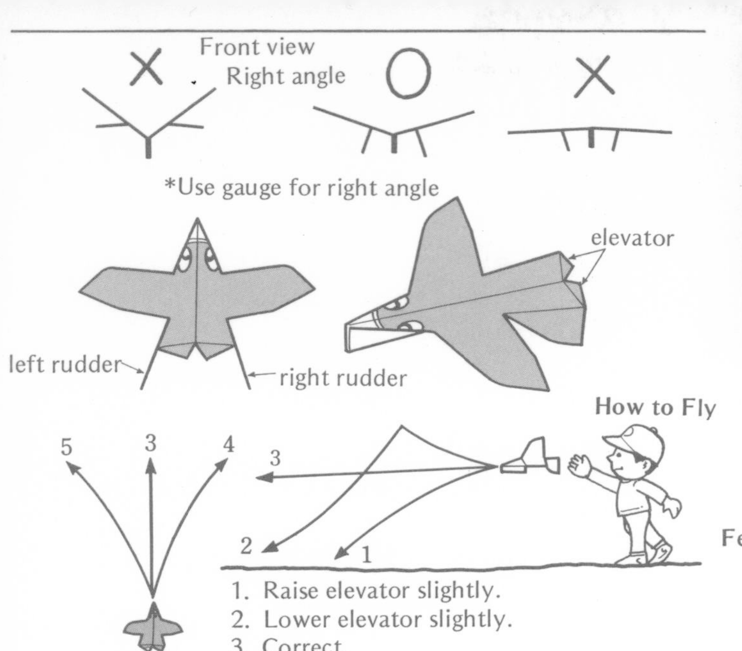

1. Raise elevator slightly.
2. Lower elevator slightly.
3. Correct.
4. Turn back of rudder to left slightly.
5. Turn back of rudder to right slightly.

*If test flight is good, launch model upward forcefully.

*Fly your model in a large area where there is no wind.

Games to Play

1. Endurance contest.
2. Longest flight.
3. Landing strip.

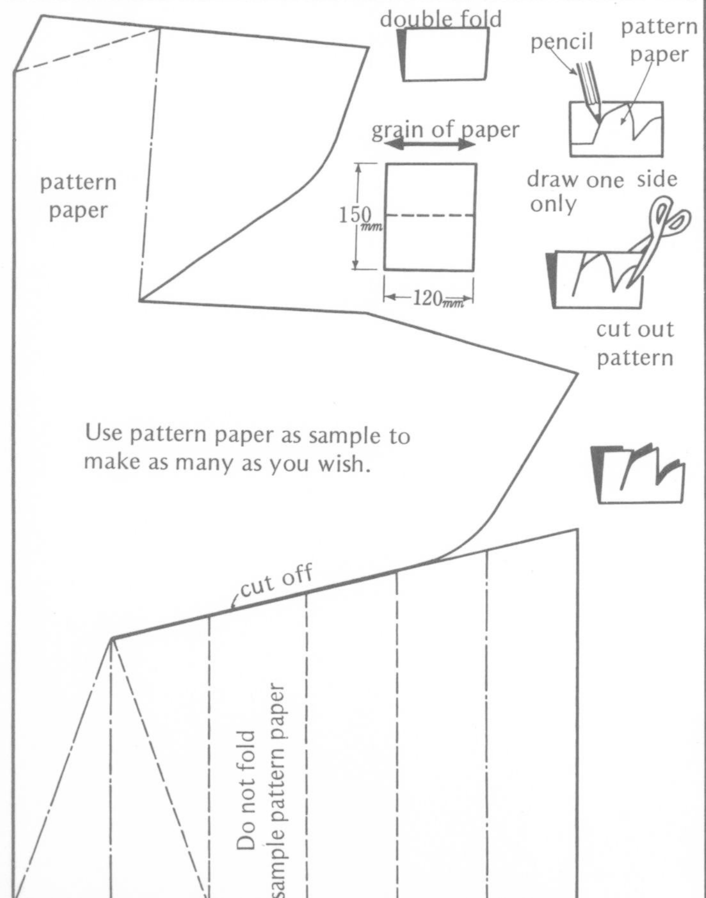

LITTLE SPARROW

Features:

1. Small area for flight.
2. No glue. Use cellophane tape or stapler to assemble.
3. Many copies may be made.

Assembly:

1. Crease fold lines with stylus.
2. Follow folding order as illustrated. Incorrect order may result in incomplete model.

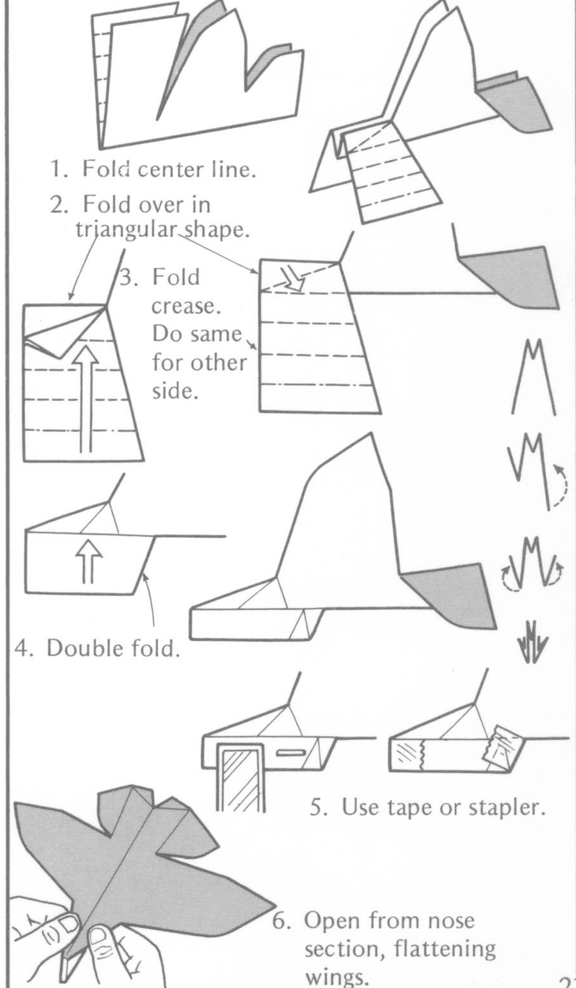

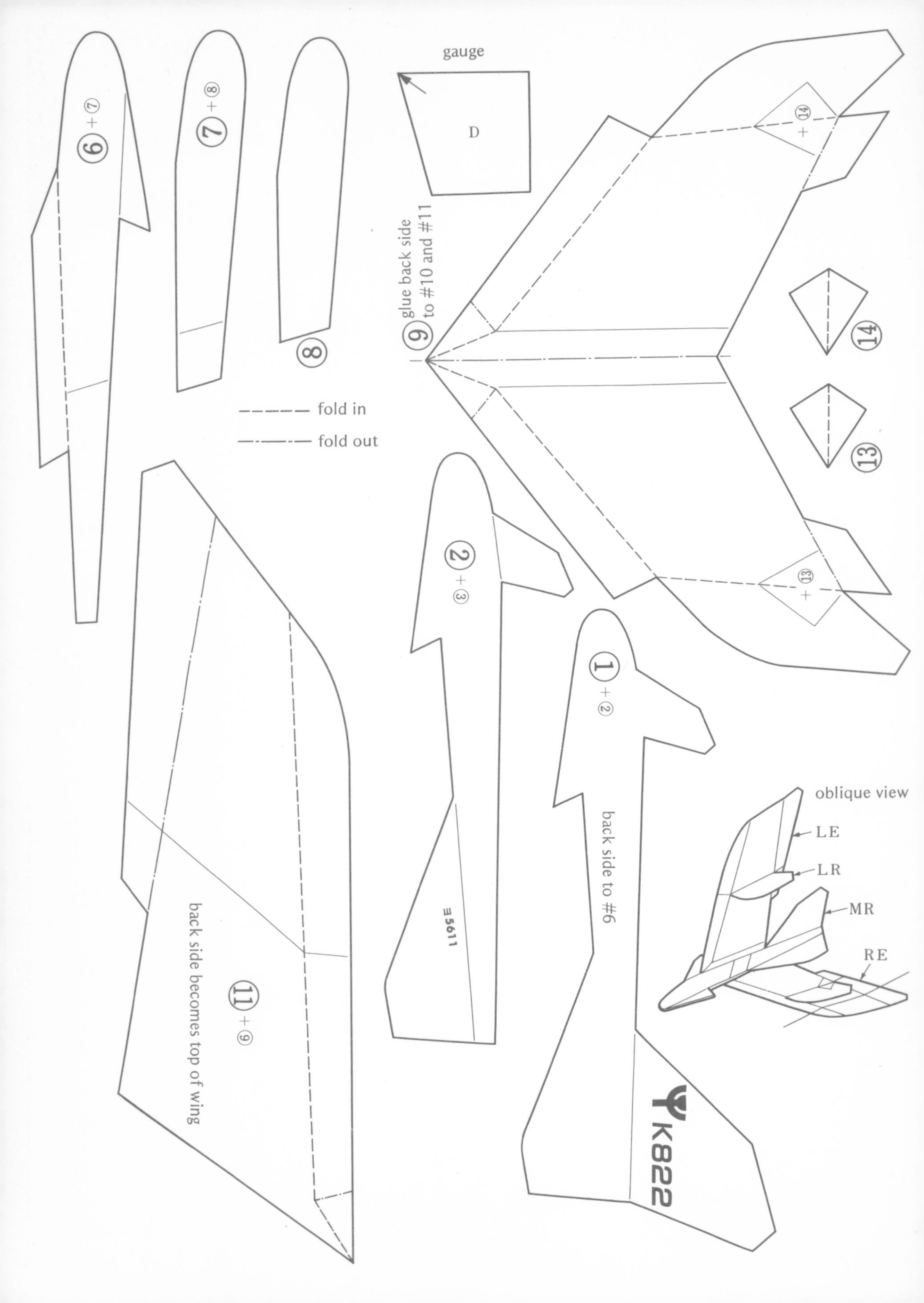

gauge
D
glue back side to #10 and #11
⑨
⑥ + ⑦
⑦ + ⑧
⑧
fold in
fold out
⑭
⑬
② + ③
① + ②
back side to #6
⑪ + ⑨
back side becomes top of wing
oblique view
LE
LR
MR
RE
K822

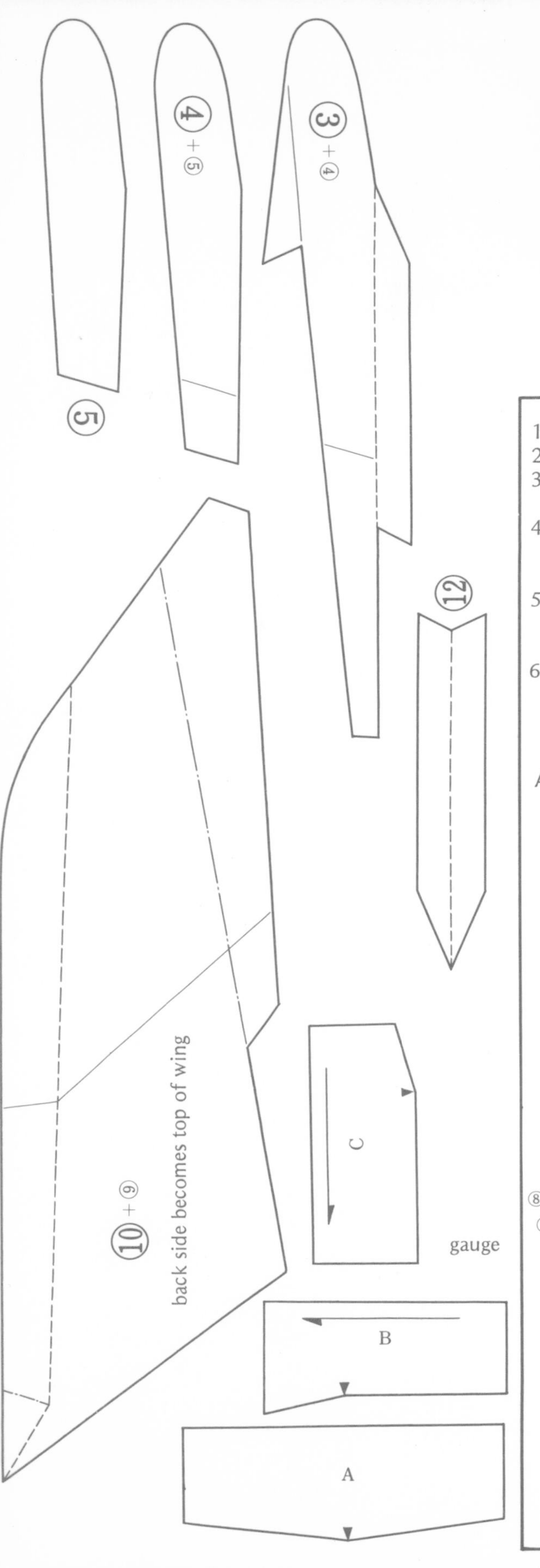

K822

1. Crease fold lines with stylus or other tool.
2. Use appropriate glue.
3. Be sure wings are on correct side. Part #12 should be attached after wings and fuselage are glued together.
4. A little twist of the wings to right or left will affect flight. Make certain they are attached correctly and at proper angle. Also, check dihedral angle with gauge.
5. If nose is too heavy, raise both sides of elevators. If nose is too light, lower elevators. Use rubber sling for launching when all tests have been completed.
6. Fly your model in safe area.

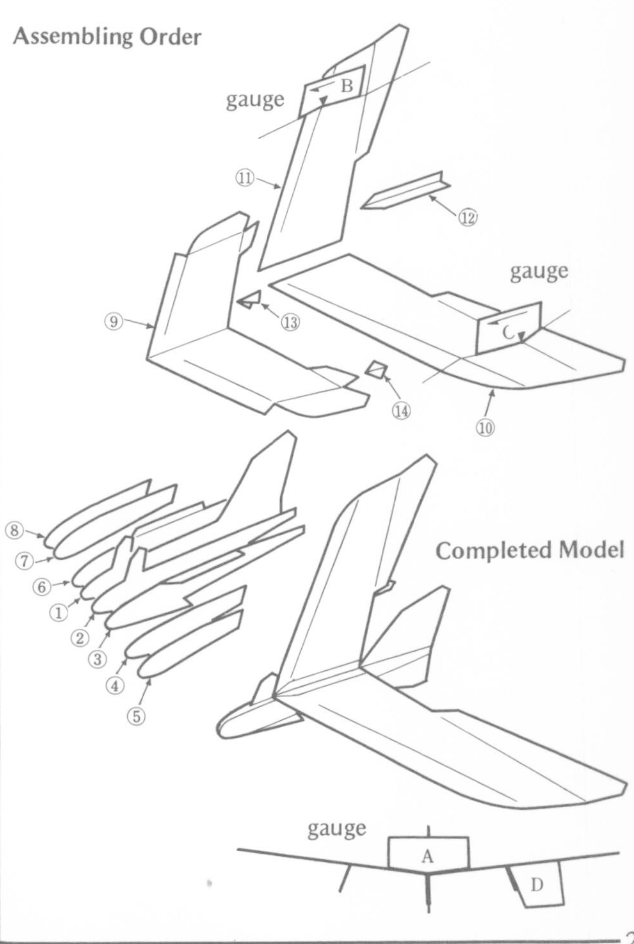

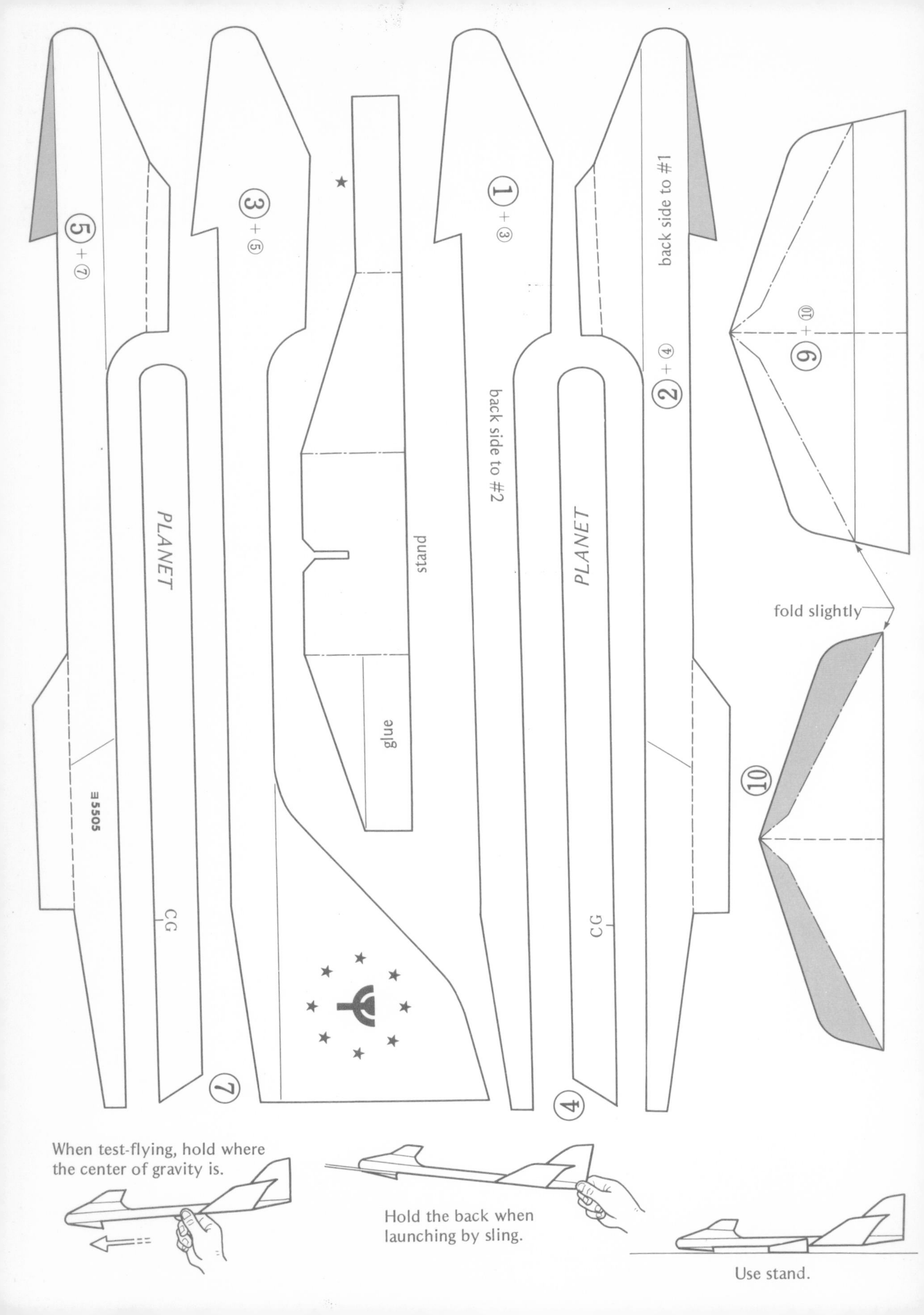

5 + 7
3 + 5
1 + 3
back side to #1
2 + 4
9 + 10
back side to #2
PLANET
PLANET
stand
glue
5505
CG
CG
fold slightly
10
7
4
When test-flying, hold where the center of gravity is.
Hold the back when launching by sling.
Use stand.

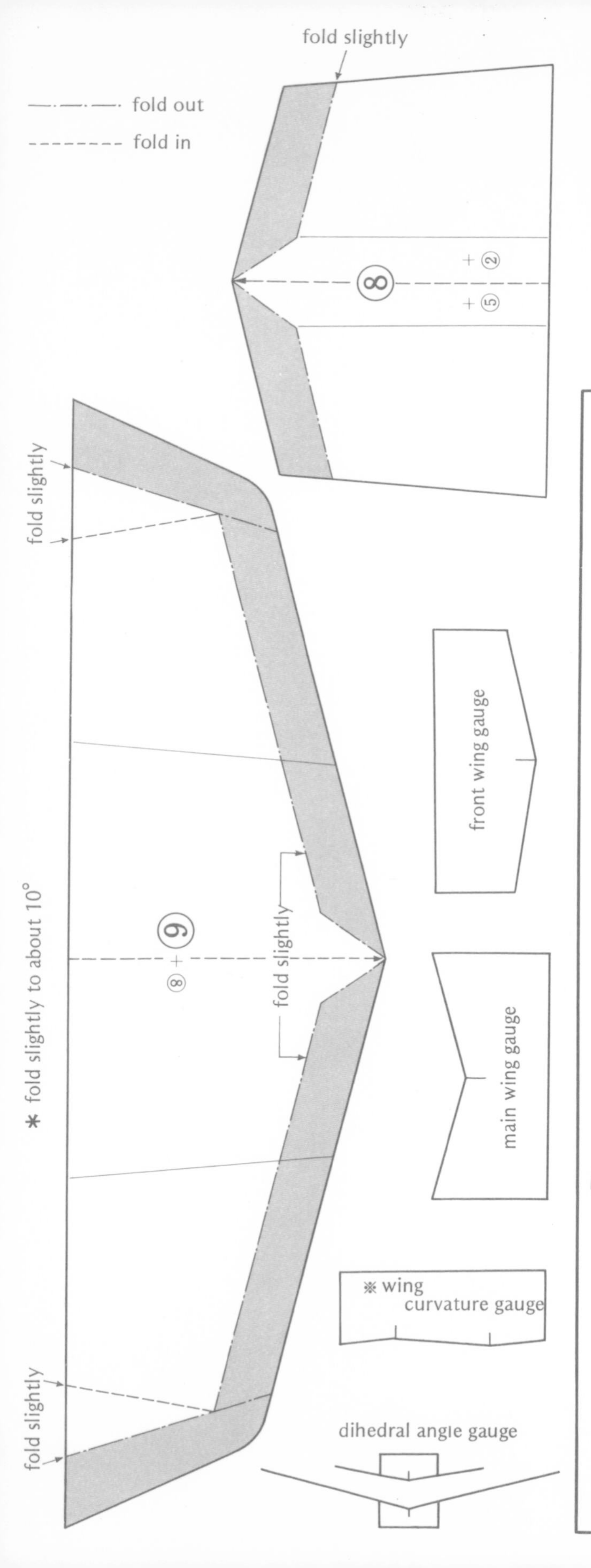

PLANET

1. Crease fold lines with stylus or other tool.
2. Use appropriate glue.
3. Correct twist and angles of fuselage and wings with gauges.
4. If nose is heavy, slightly raise front of (F), stabilizer. Do opposite if nose is too light.
5. For model to fly in left circles, lower front left section (FL) of stabilizer.
6. Use sling launching after all adjustments are made.
7. Fly your model in safe area.

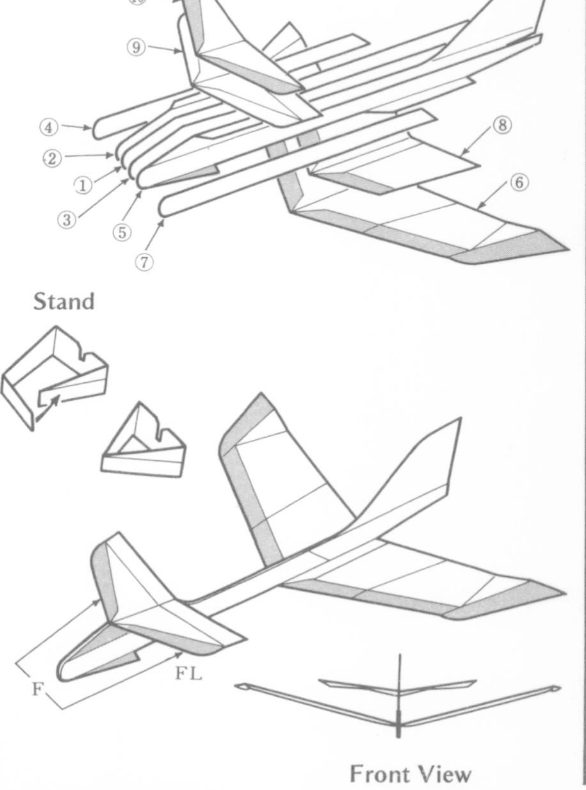

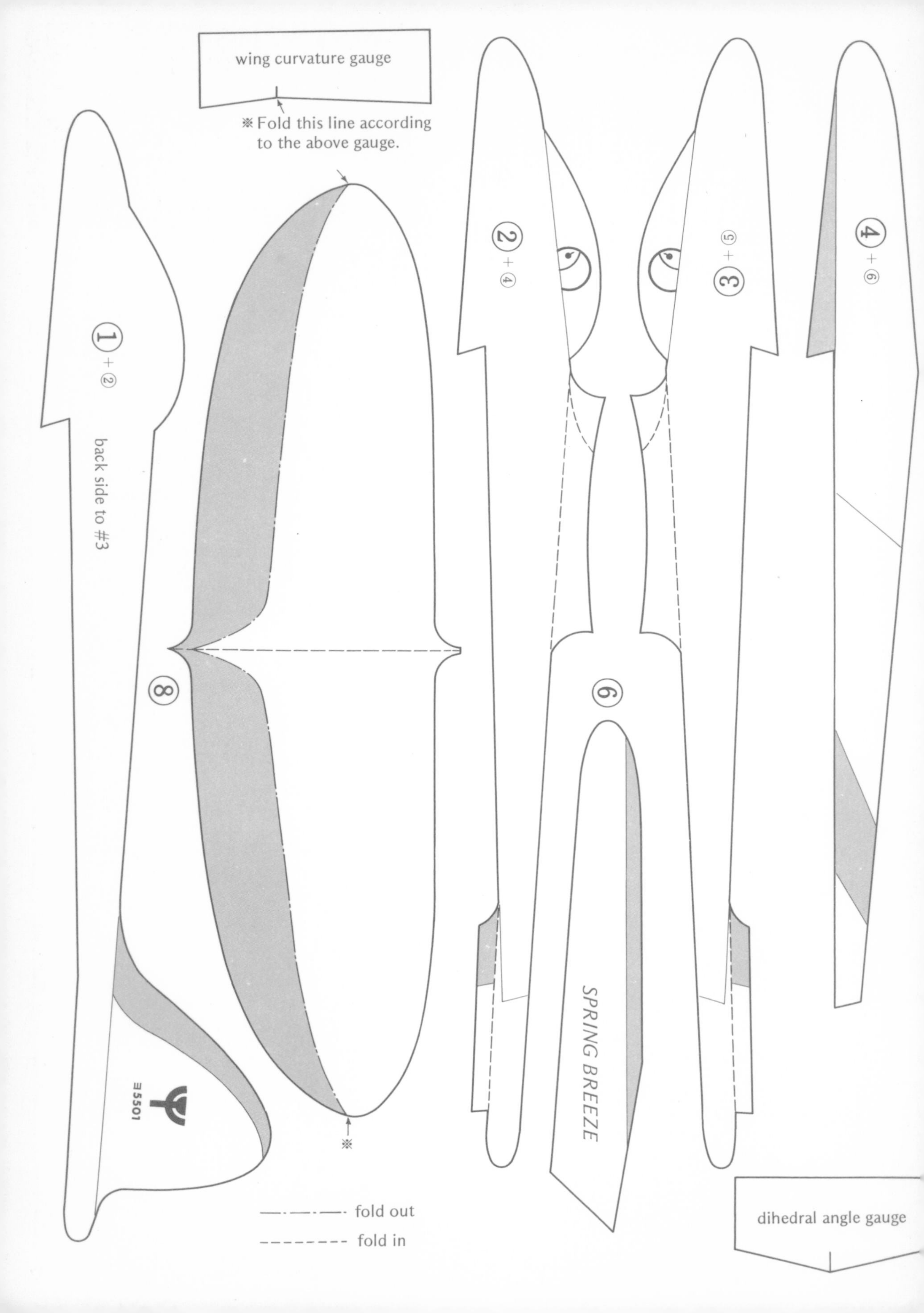

wing curvature gauge
※ Fold this line according to the above gauge.
①+②
back side to #3
⑧
②+④
③+⑤
④+⑥
⑨
SPRING BREEZE
※
5501
fold out
fold in
dihedral angle gauge

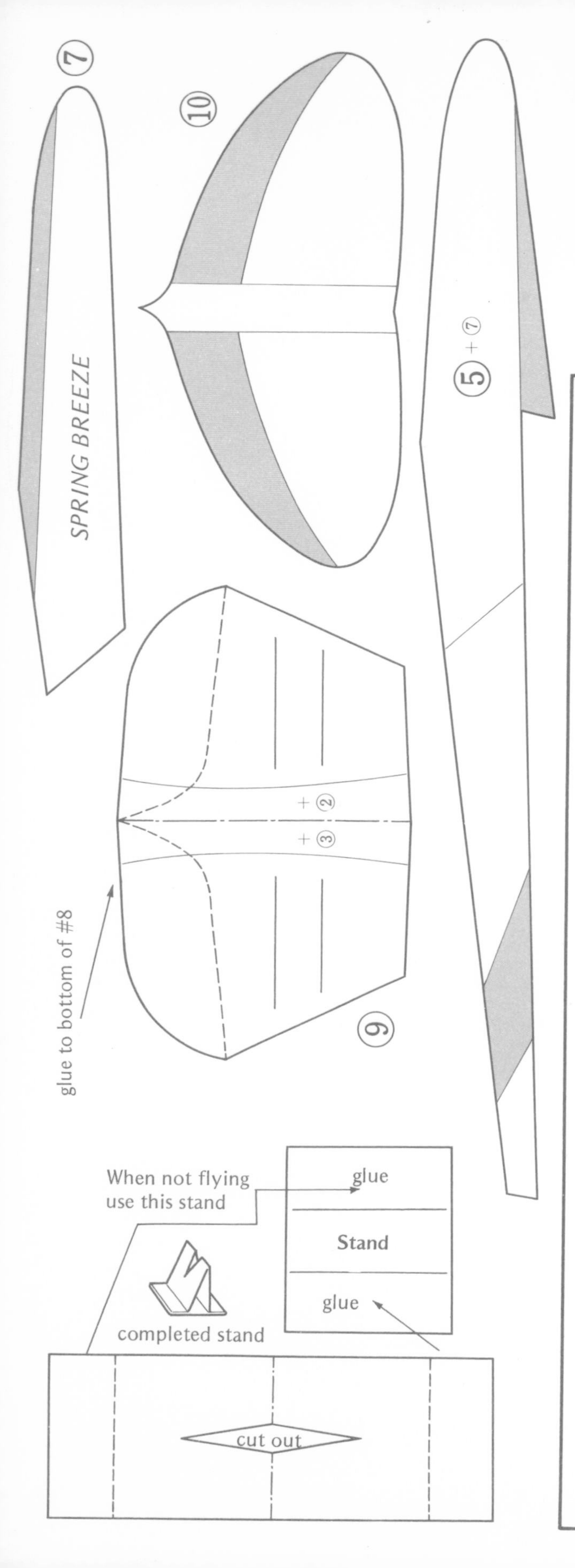

SPRING BREEZE

Features: A. Can be used for endurance flying.
B. Can be launched by sling also.

1. Crease fold lines with stylus or other tool.
2. Use appropriate glue.
3. Correct twist and angles of fuselage and wings with gauges.
4. If nose is heavy, slightly raise elevator. Do opposite if nose is light.
5. Use sling launching after all adjustments are made.
6. Fly your model in safe area.

Assembling Order

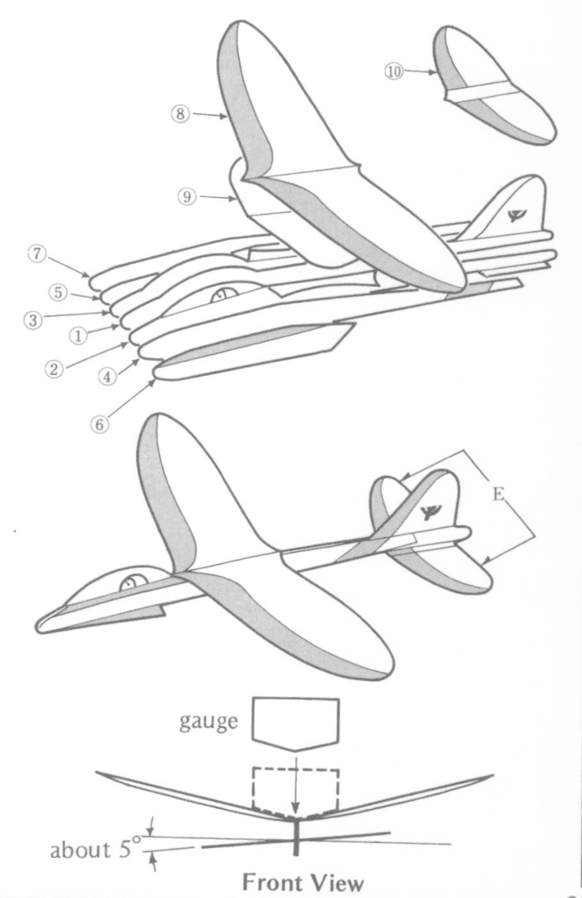

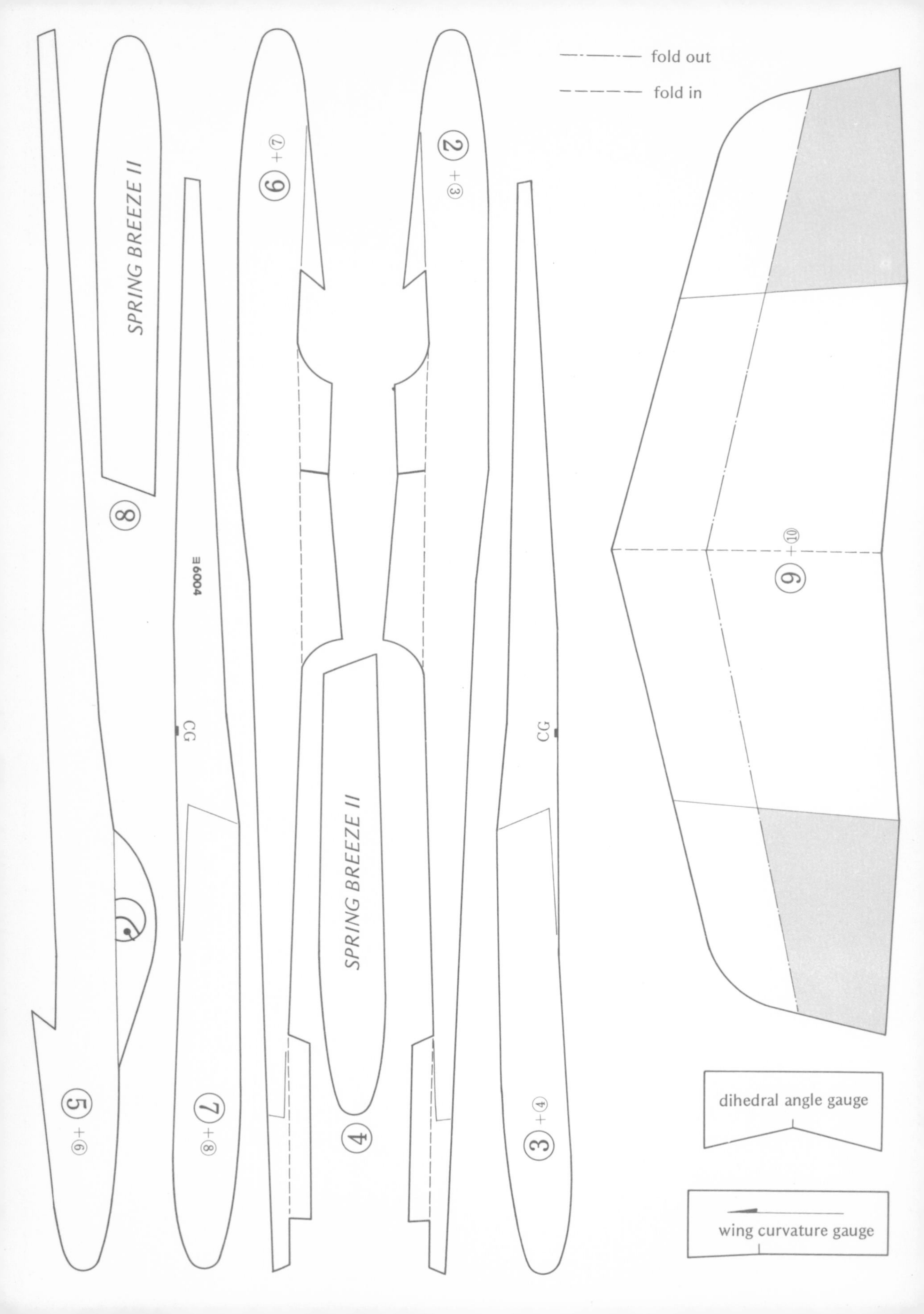
fold out
fold in
SPRING BREEZE II
SPRING BREEZE II
CG
CG
6004
dihedral angle gauge
wing curvature gauge

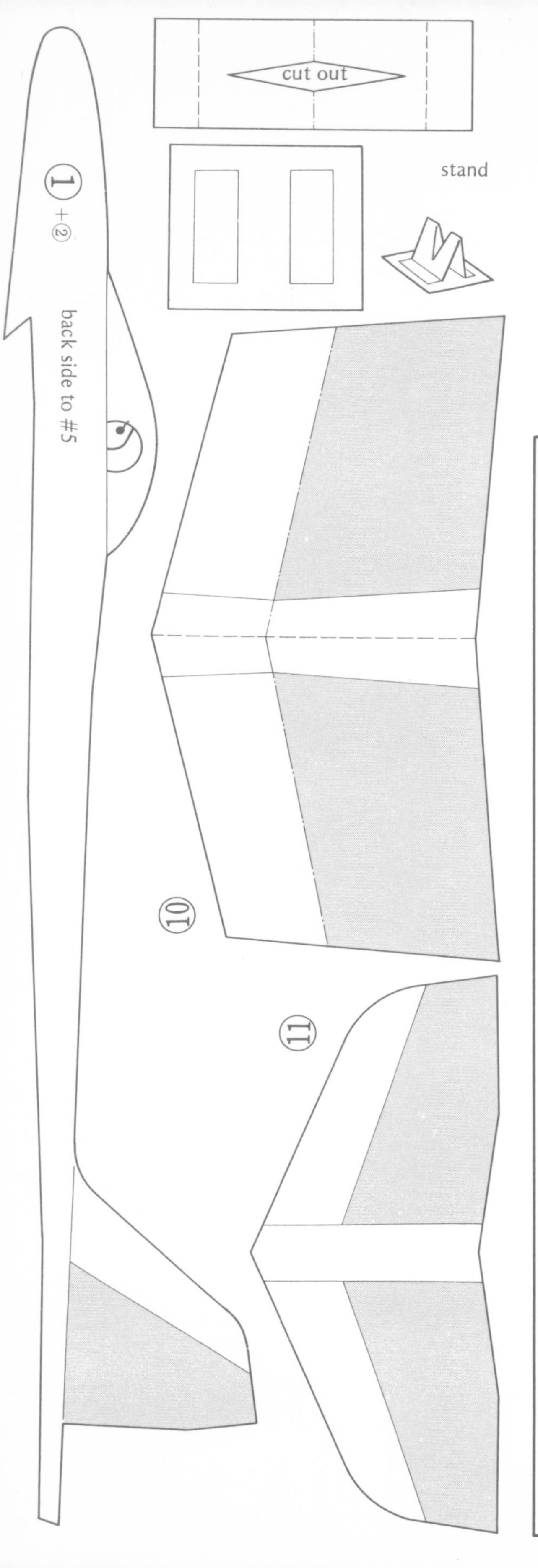

SPRING BREEZE II

1. It is important you be patient and carefully assemble your model airplane as well as make all proper adjustments. Incorrect assembly results in poor flight.
2. Crease fold lines with stylus or other tool.
3. Use appropriate glue.
4. Correct any twist in fuselage or wings. Ascertain accuracy of dihedral angle with gauge.
5. If nose is heavy, slightly raise elevator. Do opposite if nose is light.
6. Fly your model in safe area.

Assembling Order

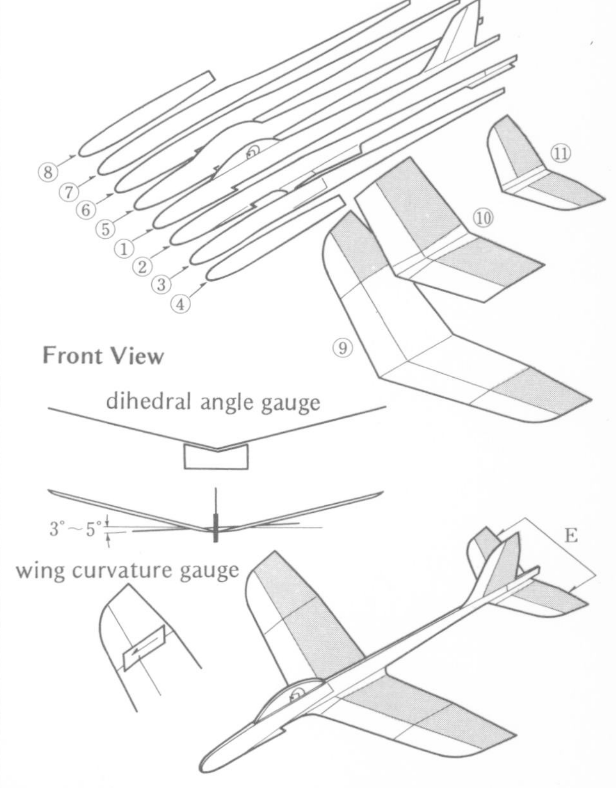

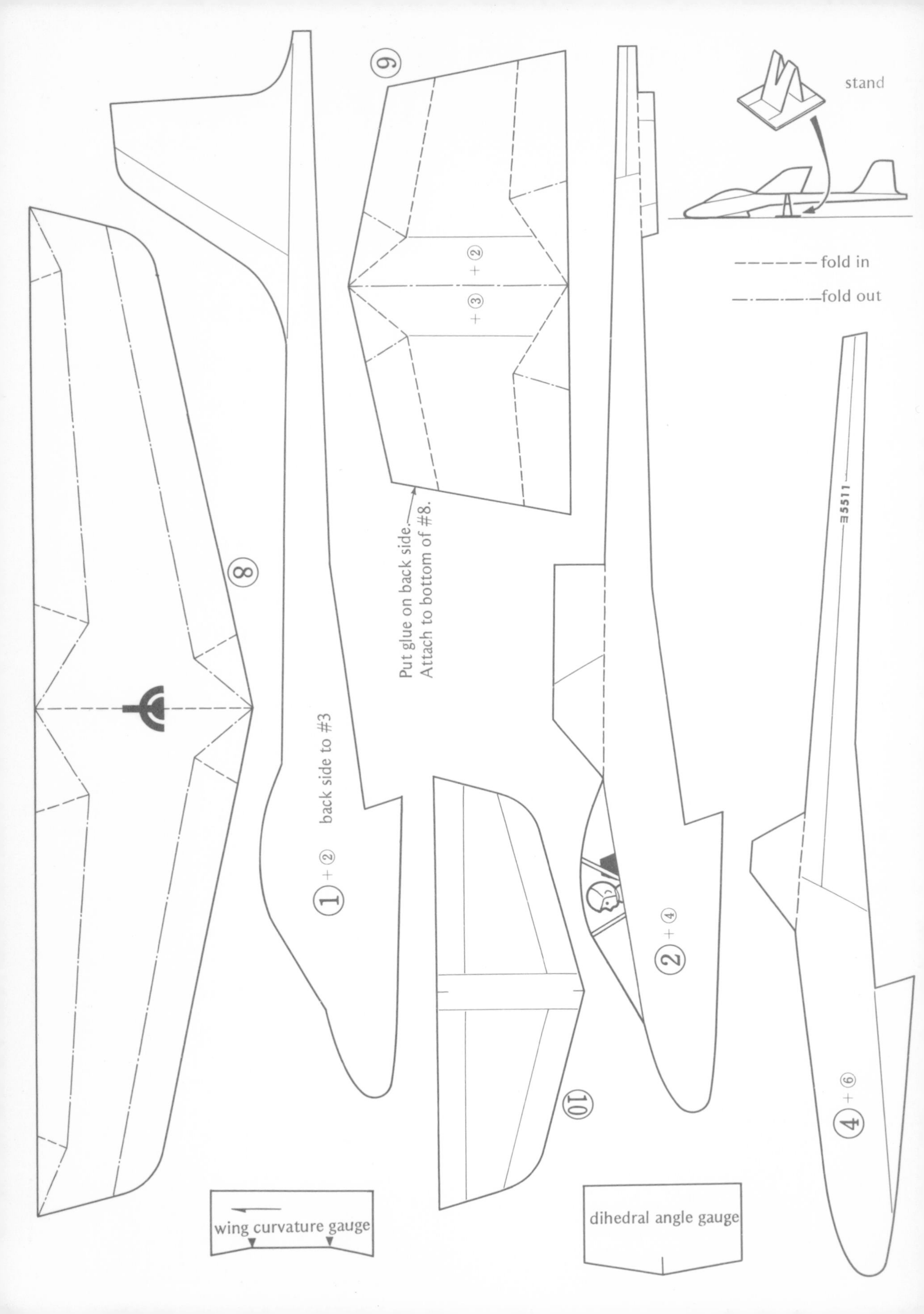
stand
fold in
fold out
9
+ 2
+ 3
8
Put glue on back side.
Attach to bottom of #8.
back side to #3
1 + 2
2 + 4
5511
4 + 6
10
wing curvature gauge
dihedral angle gauge

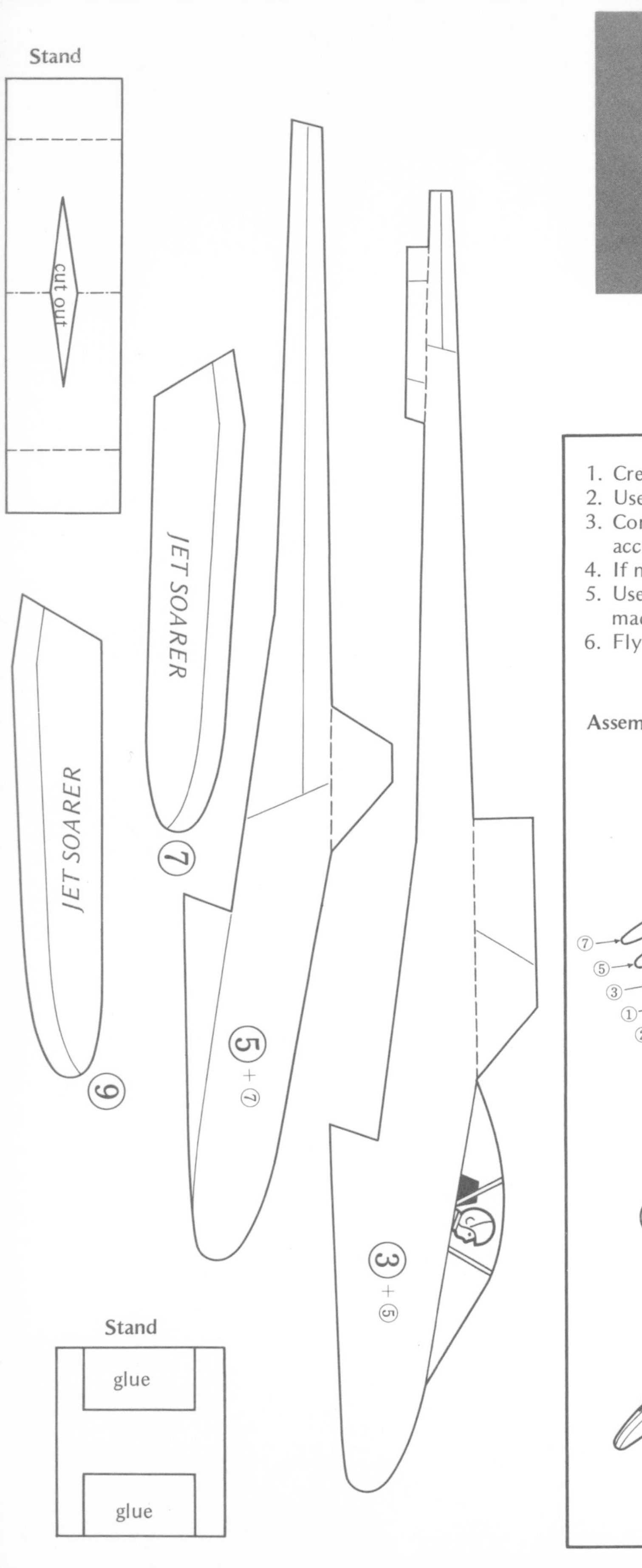

JET SOARER

1. Crease fold lines with stylus or other tool.
2. Use appropriate glue.
3. Correct any twist in fuselage or wings. Ascertain accuracy of dihedral angle with gauge.
4. If nose is heavy, slightly lower aileron area.
5. Use sling launching after all adjustments are made.
6. Fly your model in safe area.

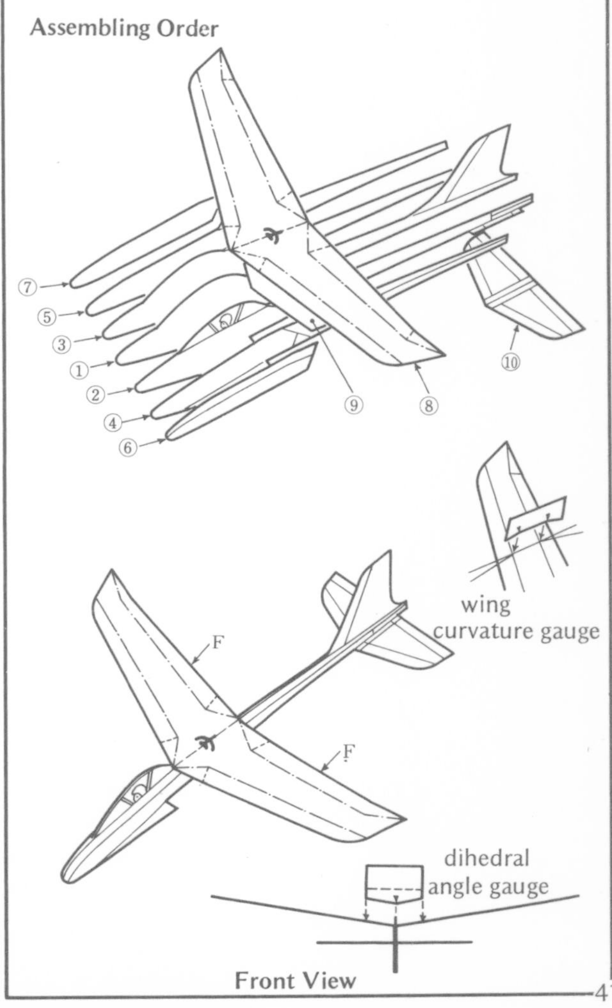

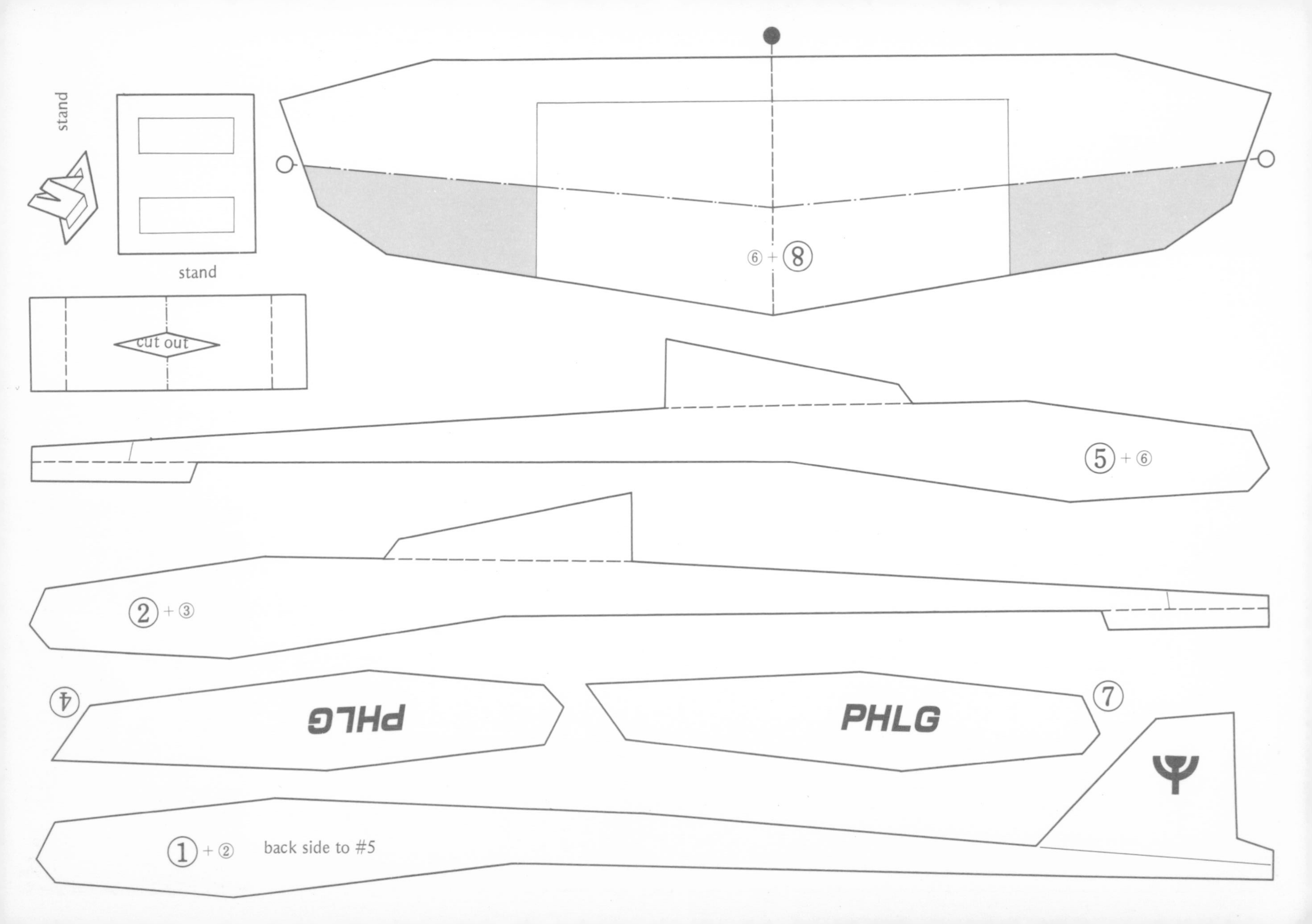
stand
stand
6 + 8
cut out
5 + 6
2 + 3
4
PHLG
PHLG
7
1 + 2
back side to #5

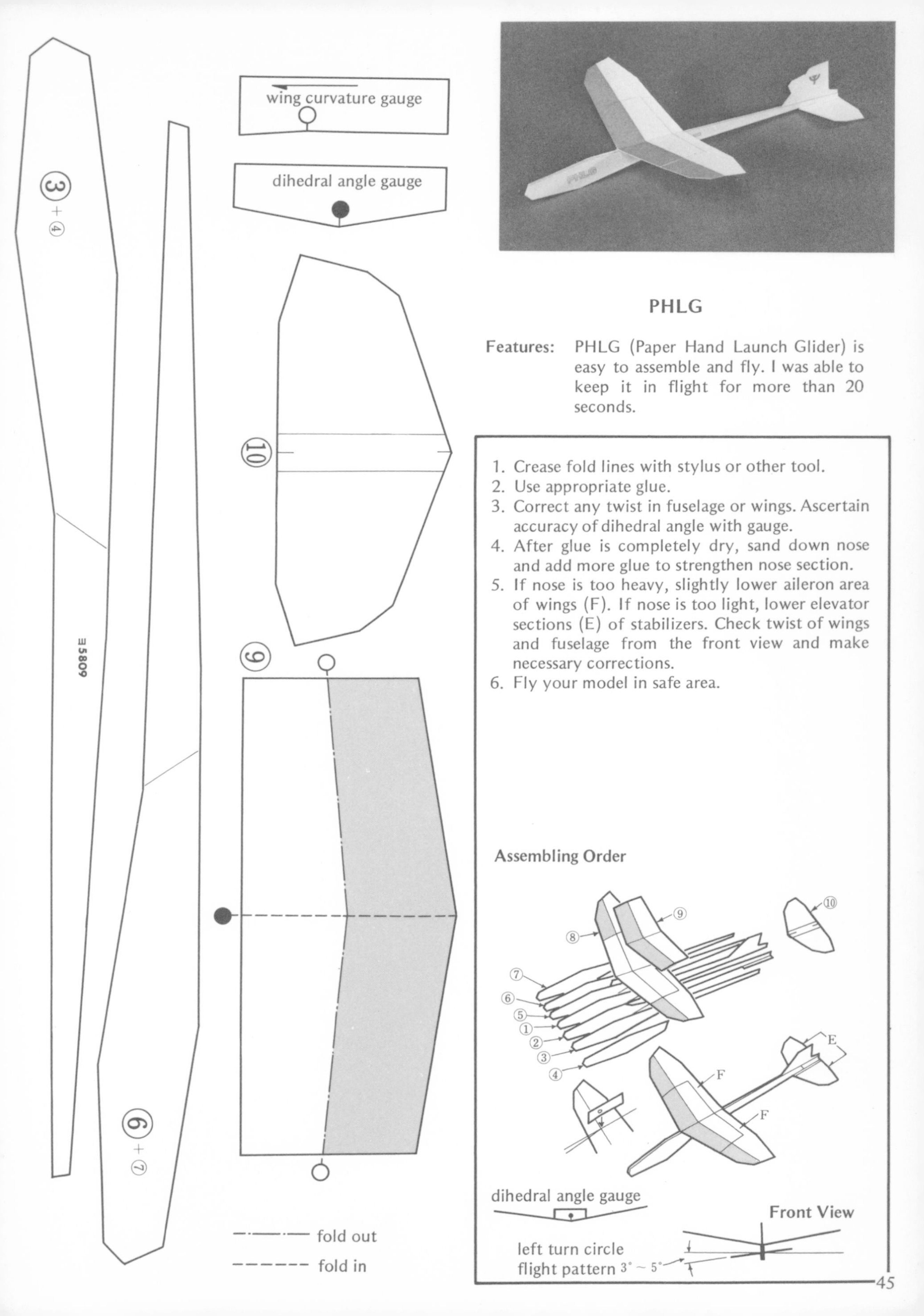

PHLG

Features: PHLG (Paper Hand Launch Glider) is easy to assemble and fly. I was able to keep it in flight for more than 20 seconds.

1. Crease fold lines with stylus or other tool.
2. Use appropriate glue.
3. Correct any twist in fuselage or wings. Ascertain accuracy of dihedral angle with gauge.
4. After glue is completely dry, sand down nose and add more glue to strengthen nose section.
5. If nose is too heavy, slightly lower aileron area of wings (F). If nose is too light, lower elevator sections (E) of stabilizers. Check twist of wings and fuselage from the front view and make necessary corrections.
6. Fly your model in safe area.

Assembling Order

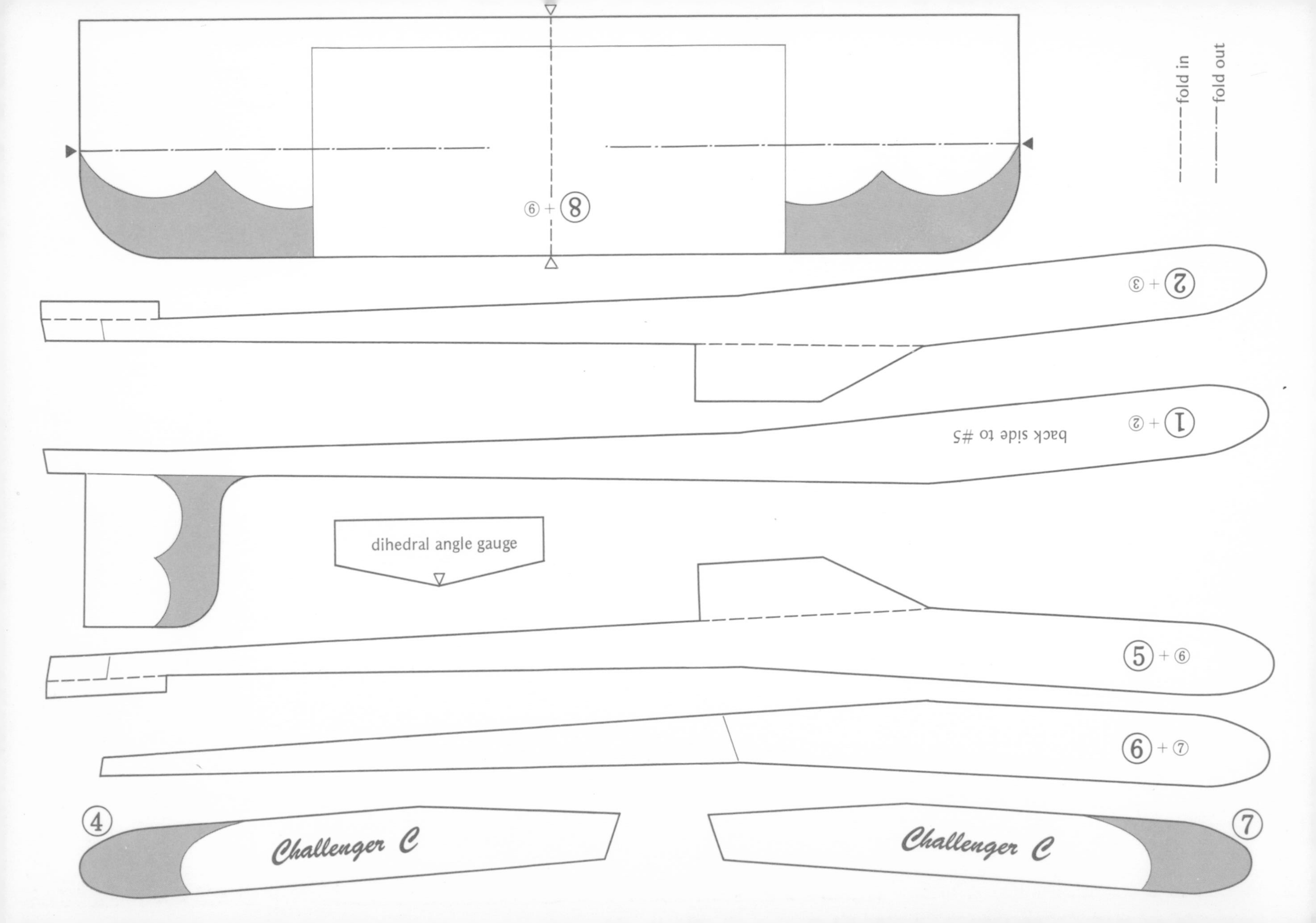

8 + 9
fold in
fold out
2 + 3
1 + 2
back side to #5
dihedral angle gauge
5 + 6
6 + 7
4
Challenger C
Challenger C
7

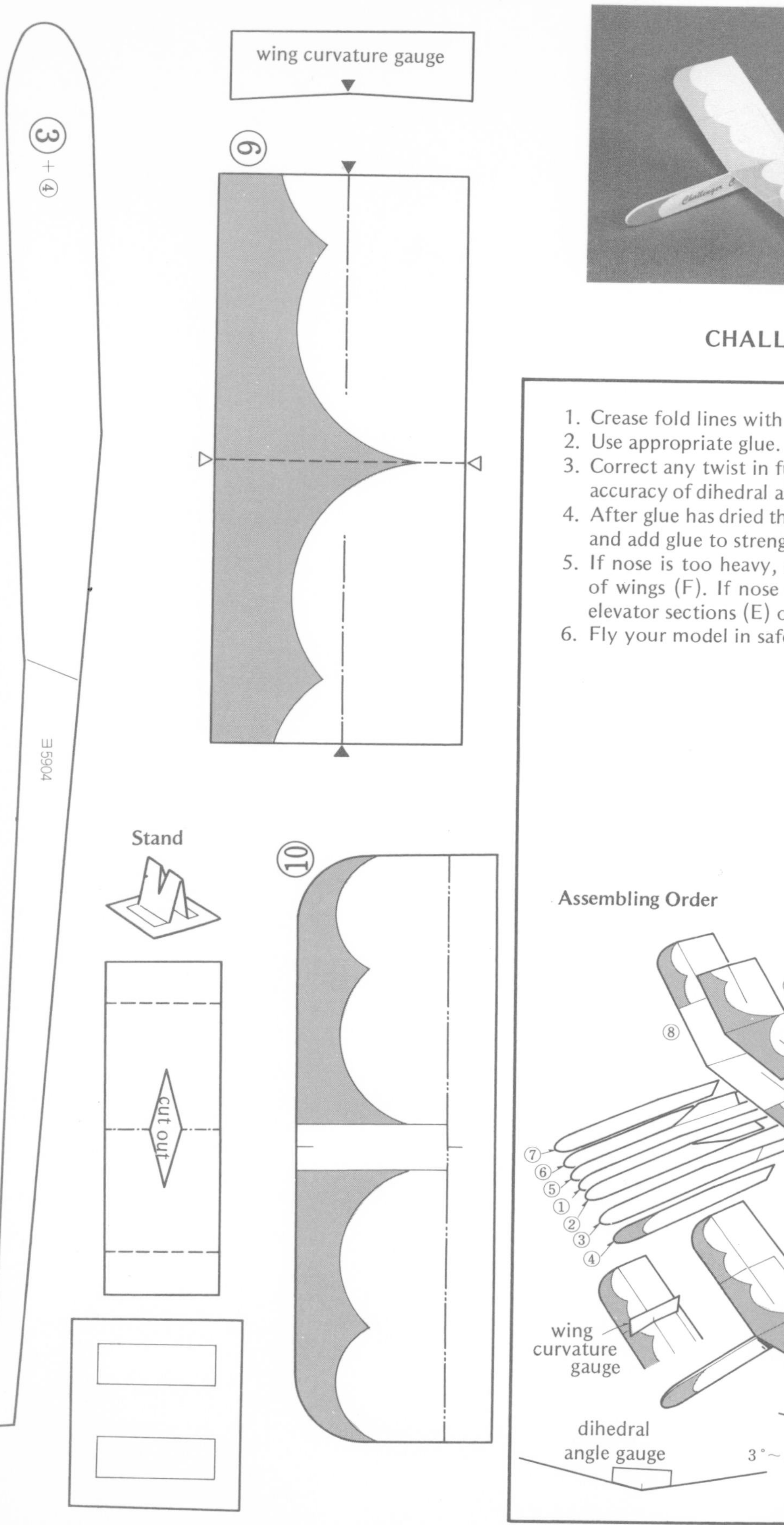

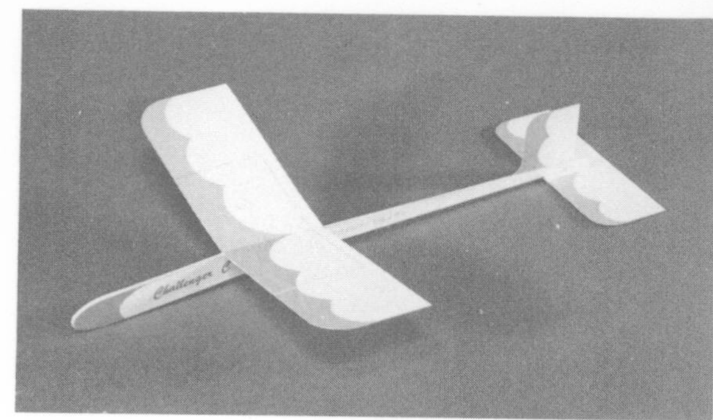

CHALLENGER-C

1. Crease fold lines with stylus or similar tool.
2. Use appropriate glue.
3. Correct any twist in fuselage or wings. Ascertain accuracy of dihedral angle with gauge.
4. After glue has dried thoroughly, sand down nose and add glue to strengthen it.
5. If nose is too heavy, slightly lower aileron area of wings (F). If nose is too light, slightly lower elevator sections (E) of stabilizer.
6. Fly your model in safe area.

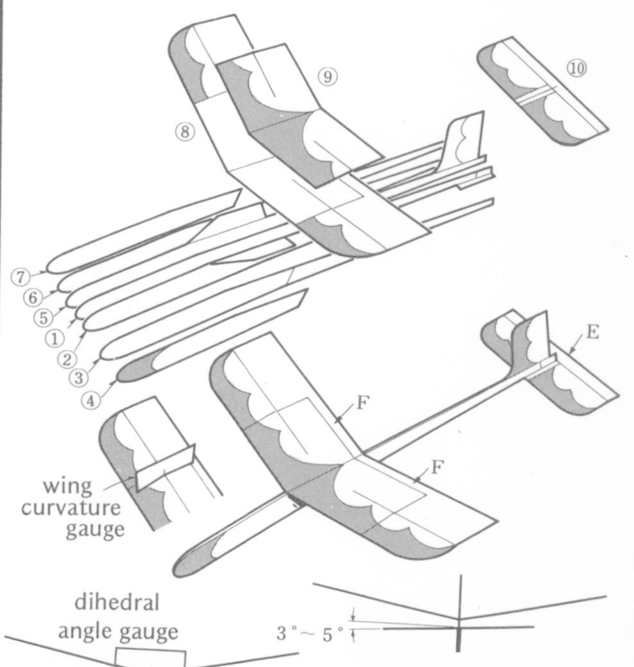

fold in
fold out
1 + 3
back side to #2
2 + 4
back side to #1
3 + 5
5 + 7
10 + 11
9 + 11
4 + 6
6 + 8
E5401

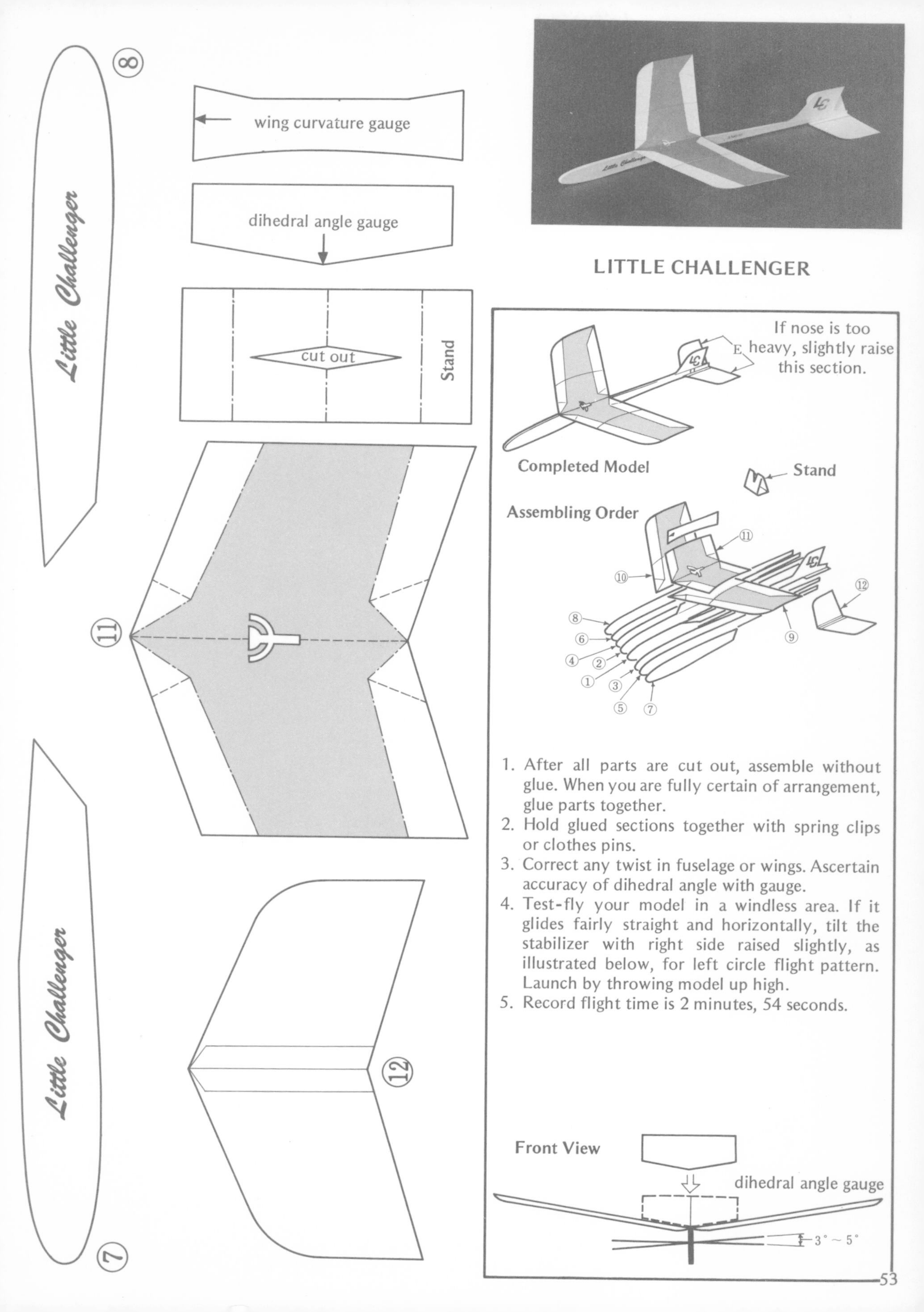

LITTLE CHALLENGER

1. After all parts are cut out, assemble without glue. When you are fully certain of arrangement, glue parts together.
2. Hold glued sections together with spring clips or clothes pins.
3. Correct any twist in fuselage or wings. Ascertain accuracy of dihedral angle with gauge.
4. Test-fly your model in a windless area. If it glides fairly straight and horizontally, tilt the stabilizer with right side raised slightly, as illustrated below, for left circle flight pattern. Launch by throwing model up high.
5. Record flight time is 2 minutes, 54 seconds.

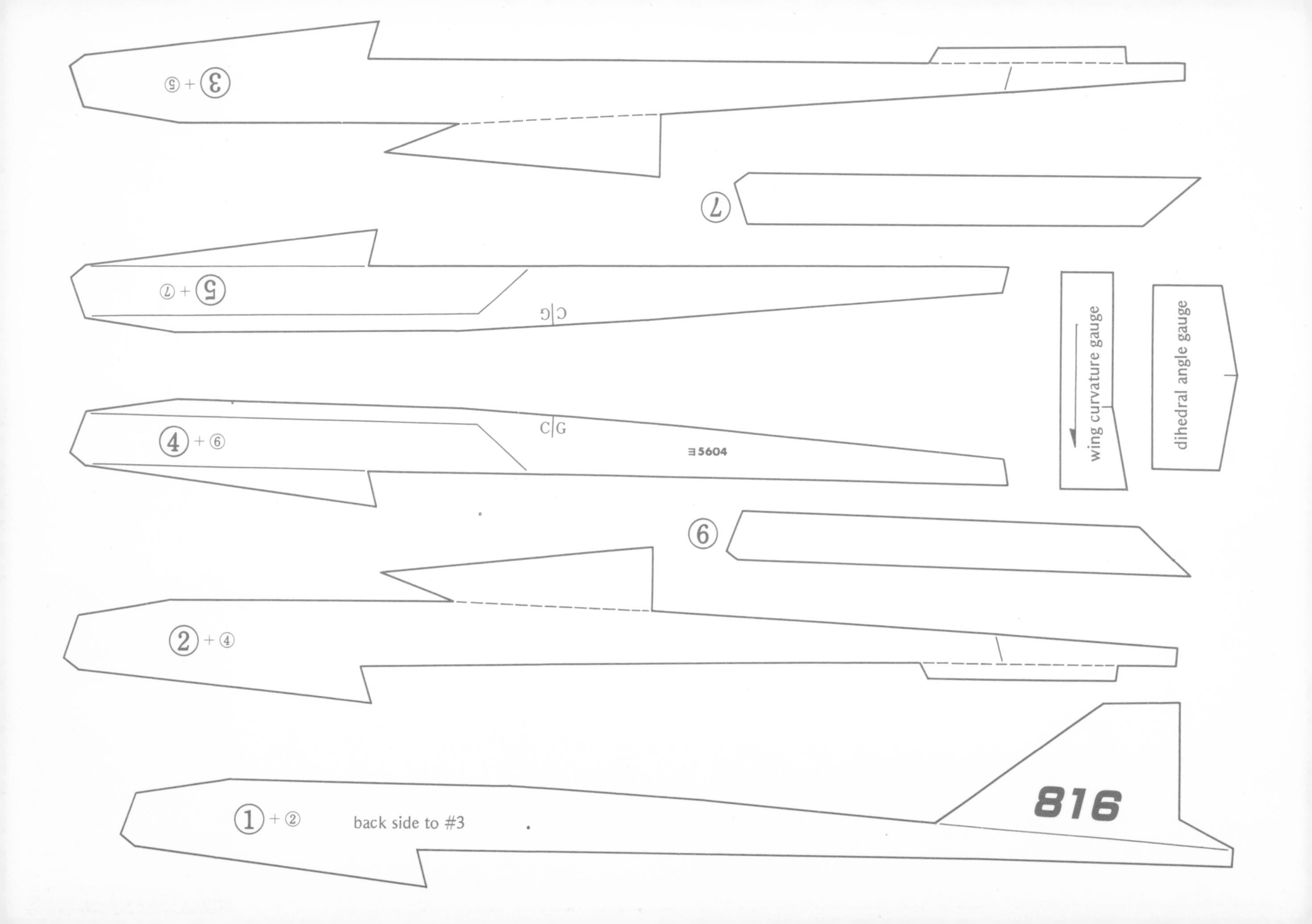

3 + 5
7
5 + 7
C|G
wing curvature gauge
dihedral angle gauge
4 + 6
C|G
5604
6
2 + 4
1 + 2
back side to #3
816

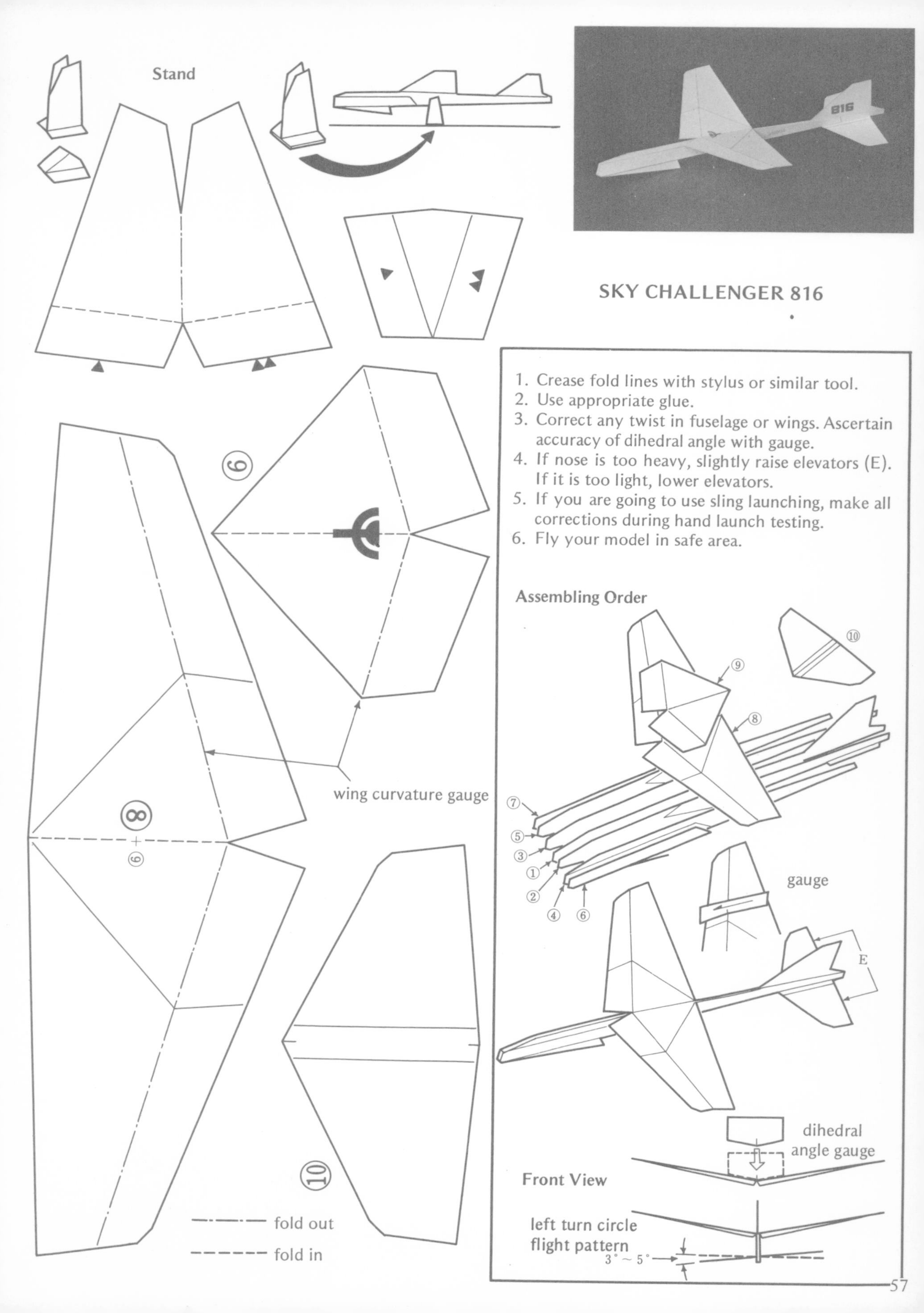
Stand
SKY CHALLENGER 816
816
1. Crease fold lines with stylus or similar tool.
2. Use appropriate glue.
3. Correct any twist in fuselage or wings. Ascertain accuracy of dihedral angle with gauge.
4. If nose is too heavy, slightly raise elevators (E). If it is too light, lower elevators.
5. If you are going to use sling launching, make all corrections during hand launch testing.
6. Fly your model in safe area.
Assembling Order
gauge
E
dihedral angle gauge
Front View
left turn circle flight pattern
3° ~ 5°
wing curvature gauge
fold out
fold in
⑥
⑧
⑨
⑩

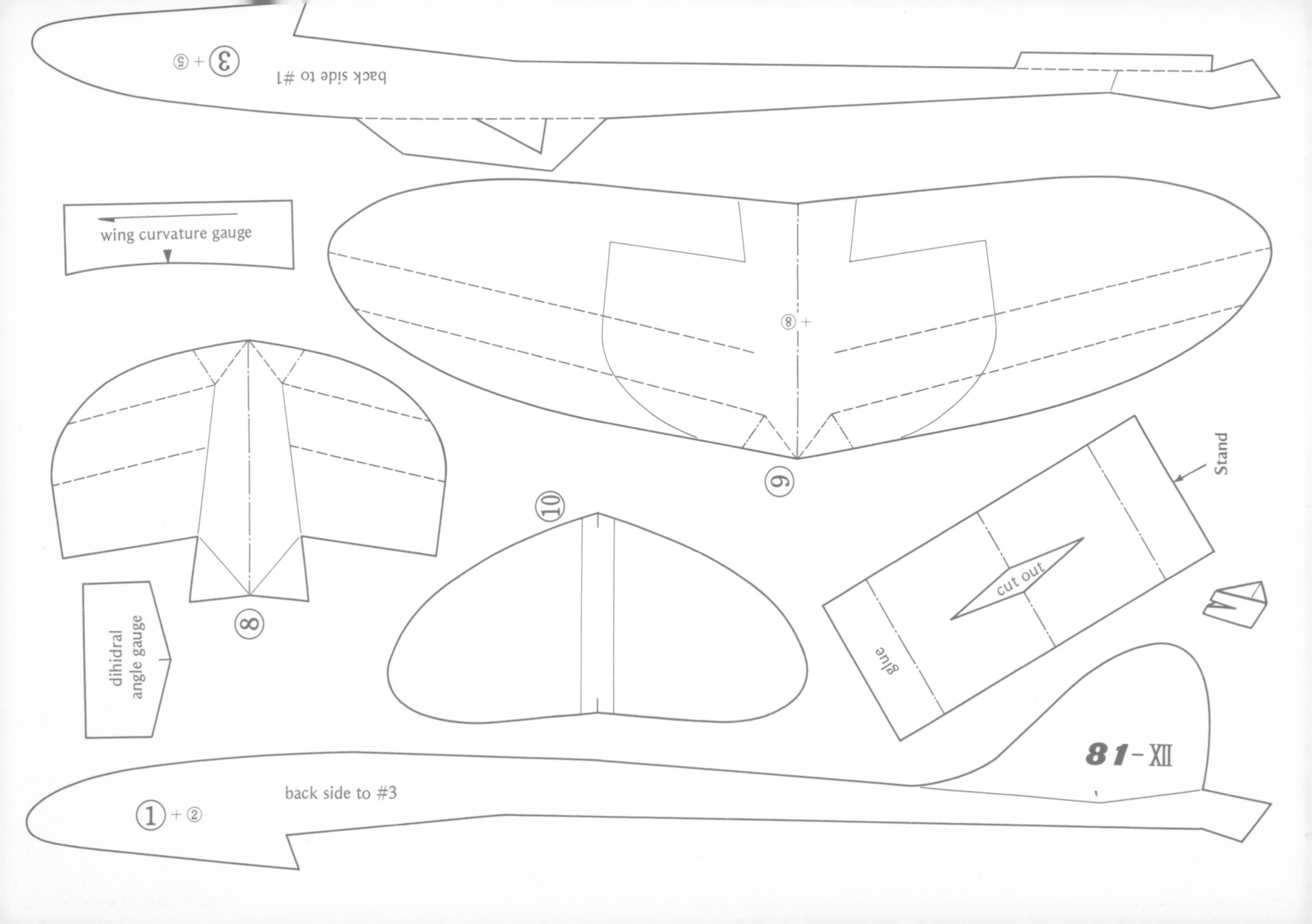
③ + ⑤
back side to #1
wing curvature gauge
⑧ +
⑧
⑨
⑩
Stand
cut out
glue
dihidral
angle gauge
81-XII
① + ②
back side to #3

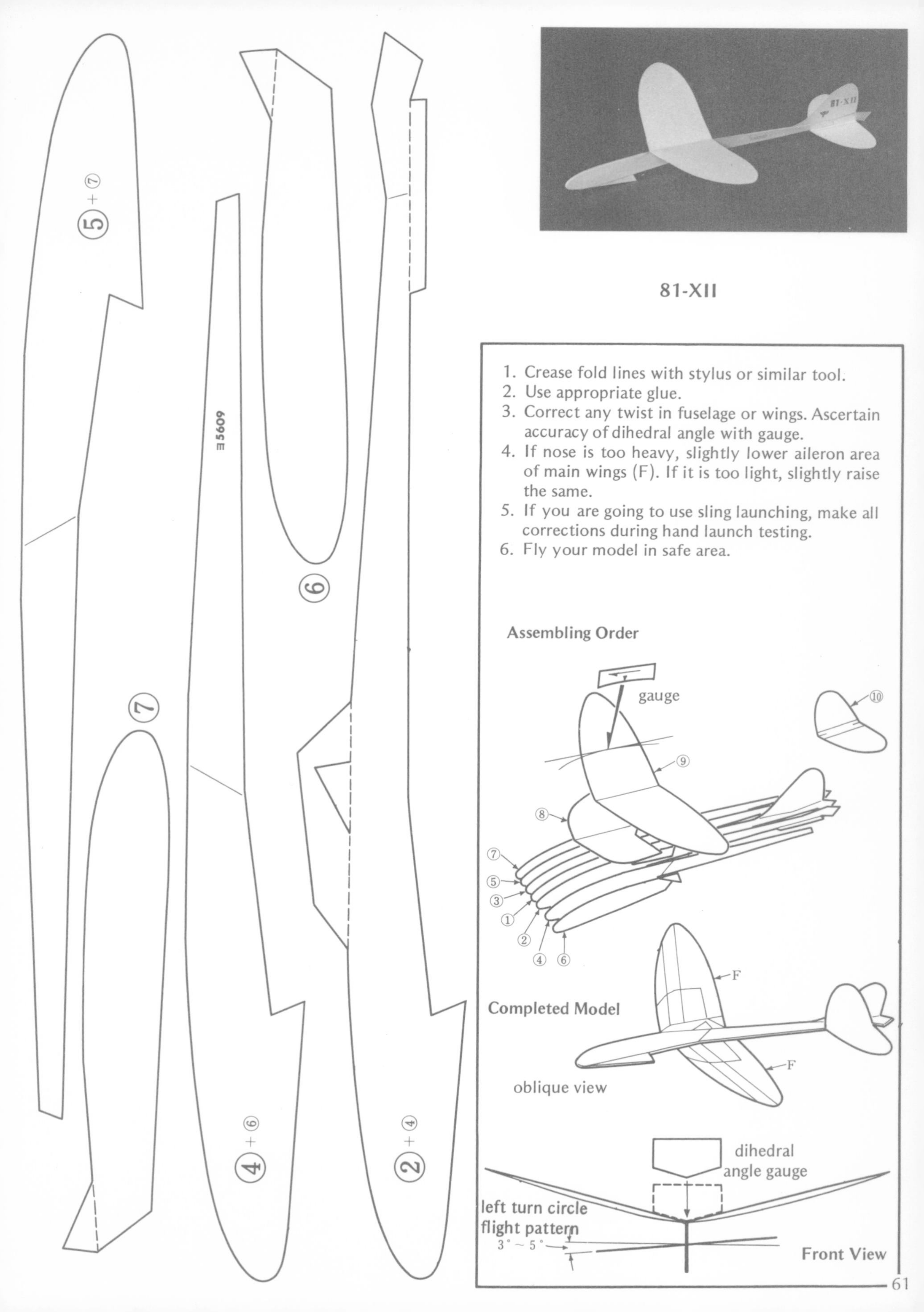

81-XII

1. Crease fold lines with stylus or similar tool.
2. Use appropriate glue.
3. Correct any twist in fuselage or wings. Ascertain accuracy of dihedral angle with gauge.
4. If nose is too heavy, slightly lower aileron area of main wings (F). If it is too light, slightly raise the same.
5. If you are going to use sling launching, make all corrections during hand launch testing.
6. Fly your model in safe area.

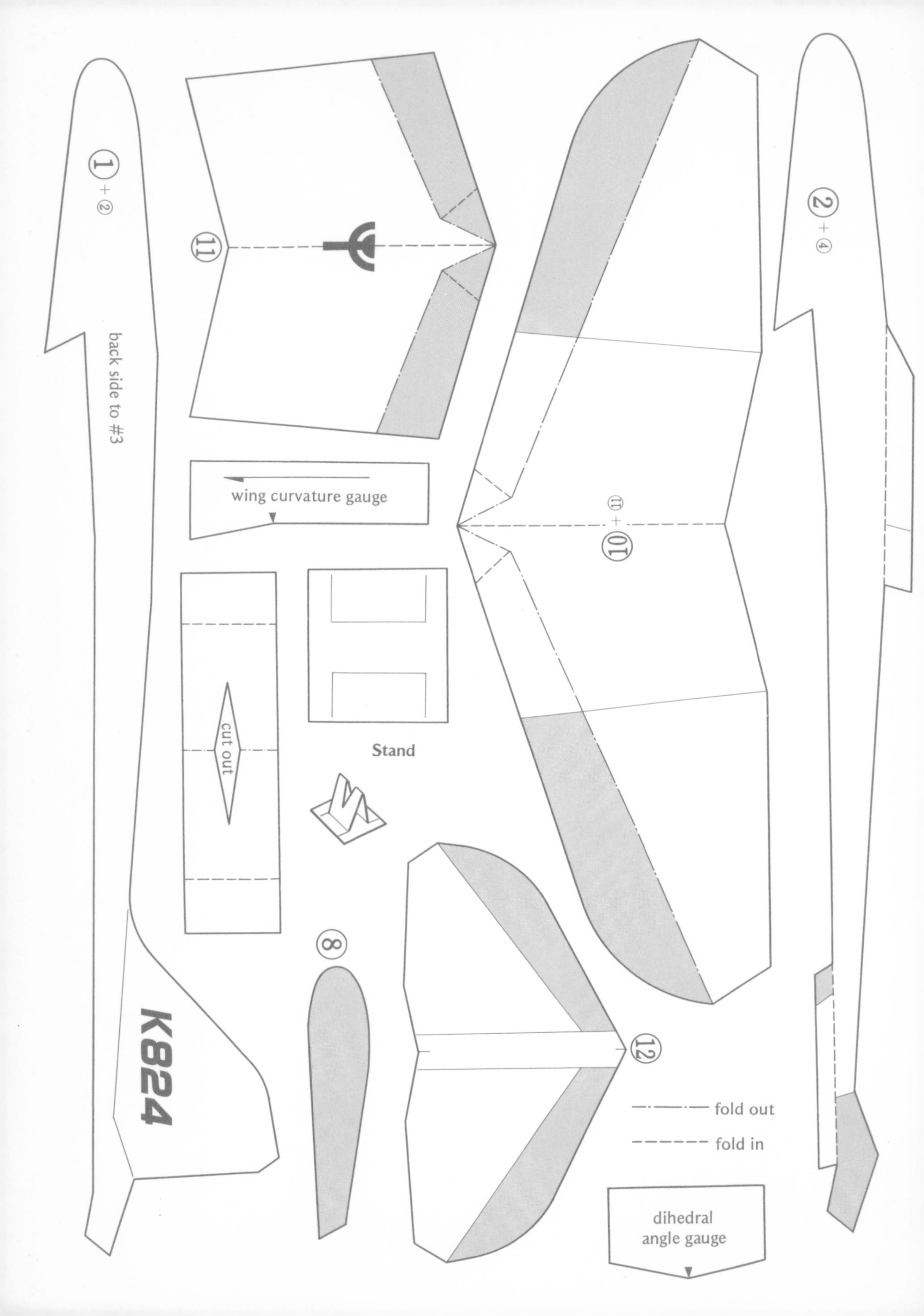

1 + 2
back side to #3
2 + 4
11
10 + 11
wing curvature gauge
cut out
Stand
K824
8
12
fold out
fold in
dihedral
angle gauge

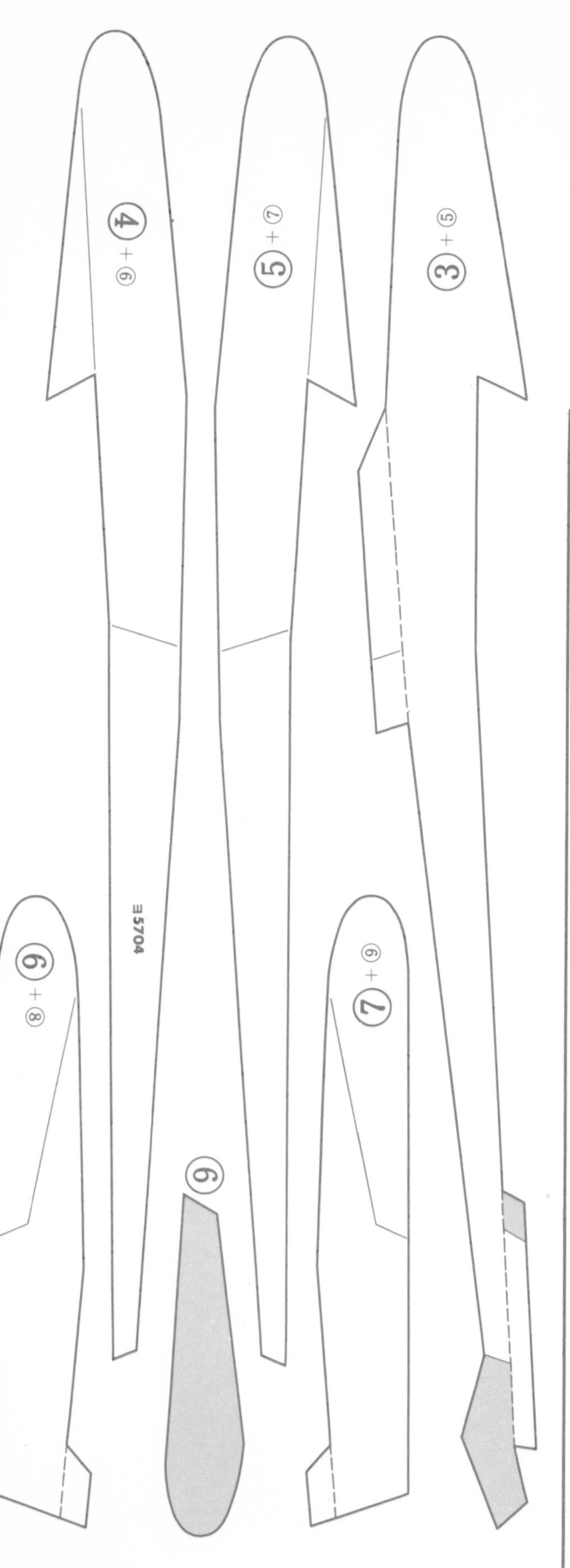

K824

1. Crease fold lines with stylus or similar tool.
2. Use appropriate glue.
3. Correct any twist in fuselage or wings. Ascertain accuracy of dihedral angle with gauge.
4. If nose is too heavy, slightly lower aileron area of main wings (F). If it is too light, slightly lower elevators (E).
5. If you are going to use sling launching, make all corrections during hand launch testing.
6. Fly your model in safe area.

Assembling Order

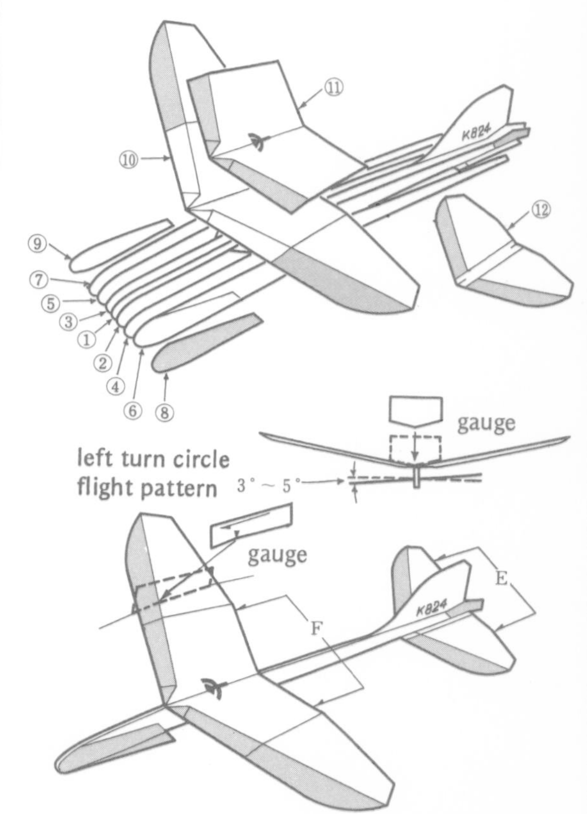

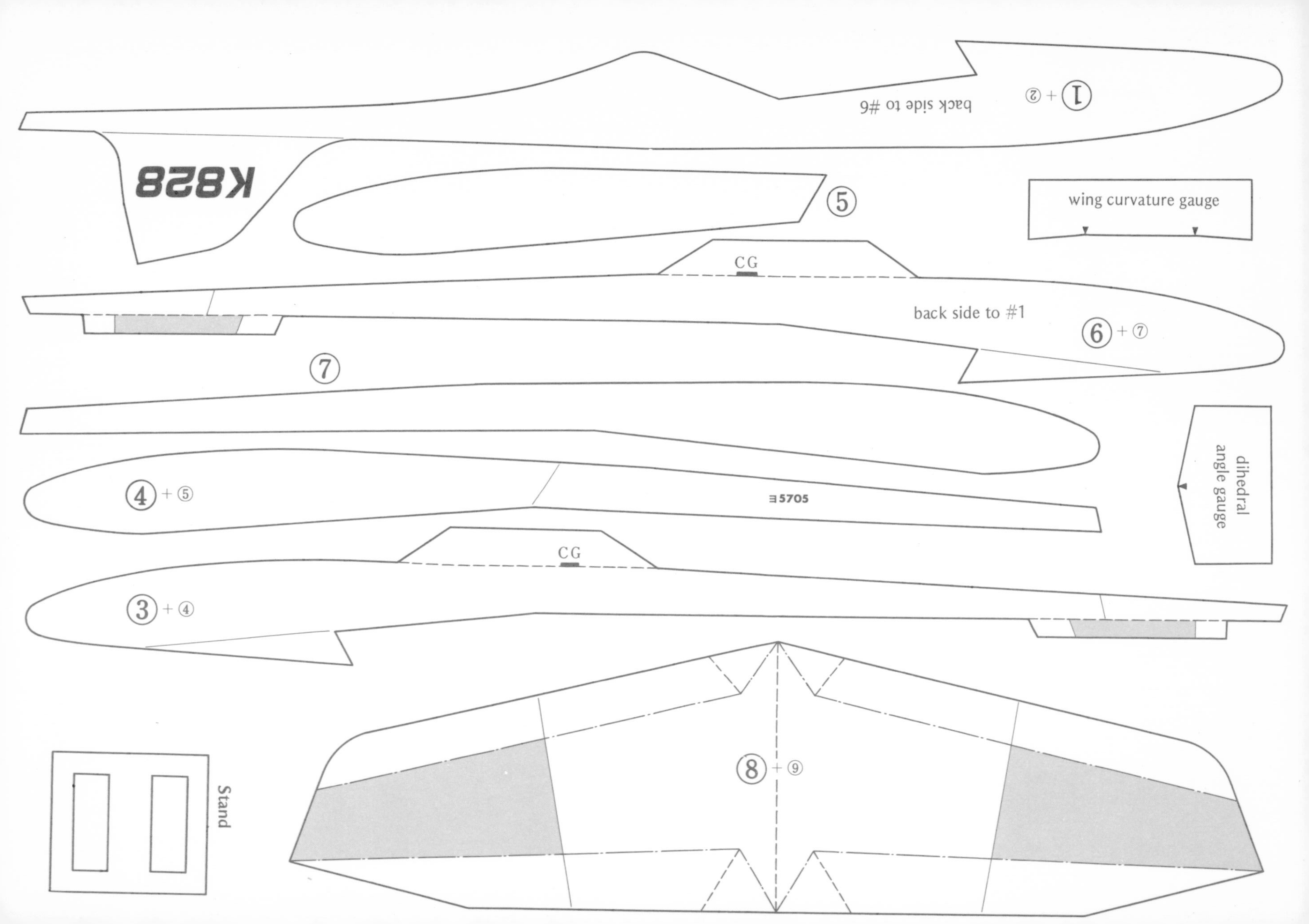

back side to #6
1 + 2
K828
5
wing curvature gauge
CG
back side to #1
6 + 7
7
dihedral
angle gauge
4 + 5
5705
CG
3 + 4
8 + 9
Stand

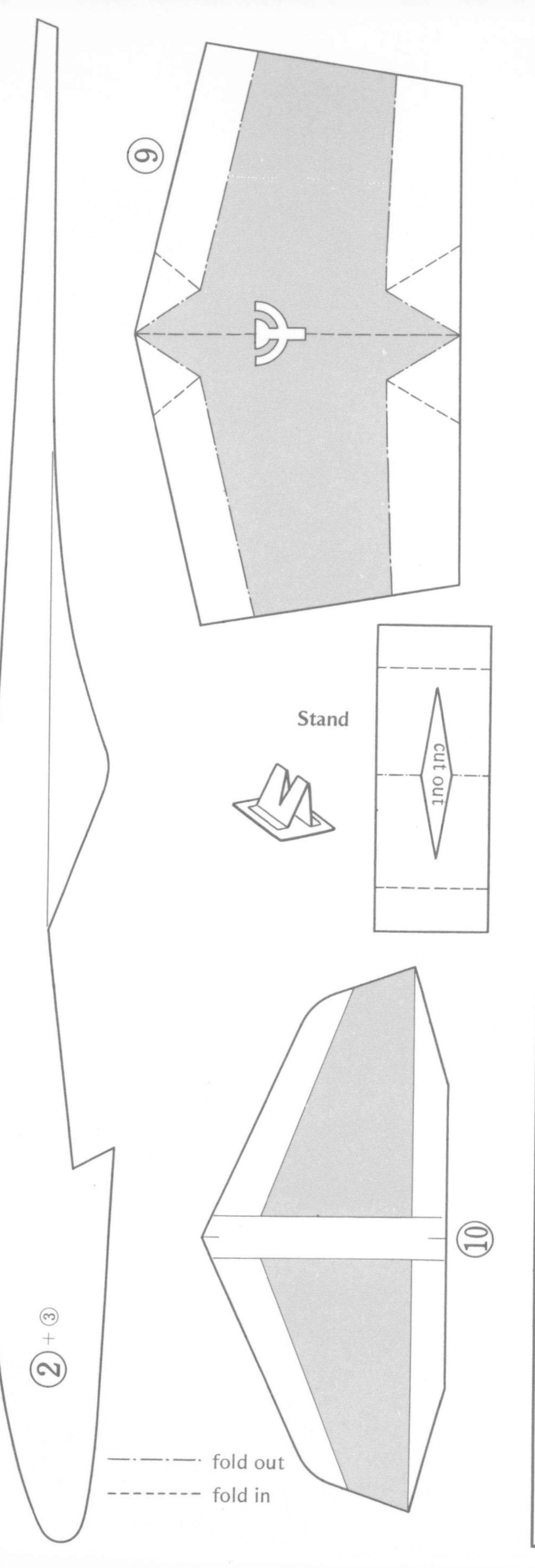

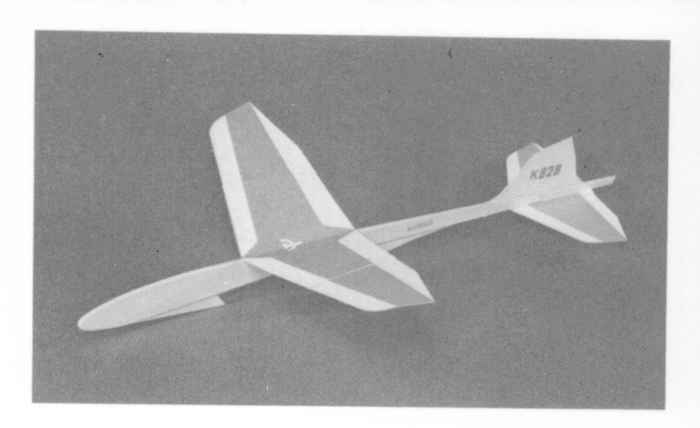

K828

1. Crease fold lines with stylus or similar tool.
2. Use appropriate glue.
3. Correct any twist in fuselage or wings. Ascertain accuracy of dihedral angle with gauge.
4. If nose is too heavy, slightly lower aileron area of main wings (F). If it is too light, slightly lower elevators (E).
5. If you are going to use sling launching, make all corrections during hand launch testing.
6. Fly your model in safe area.

Assembling Order

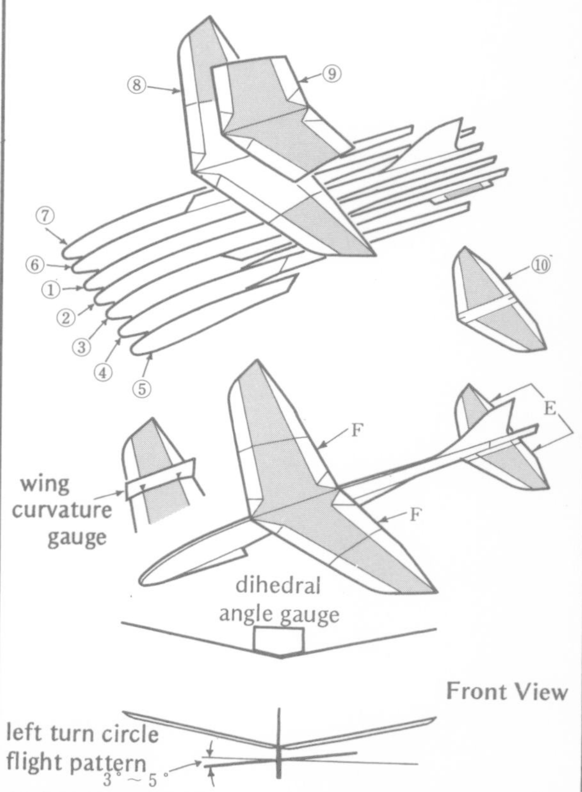

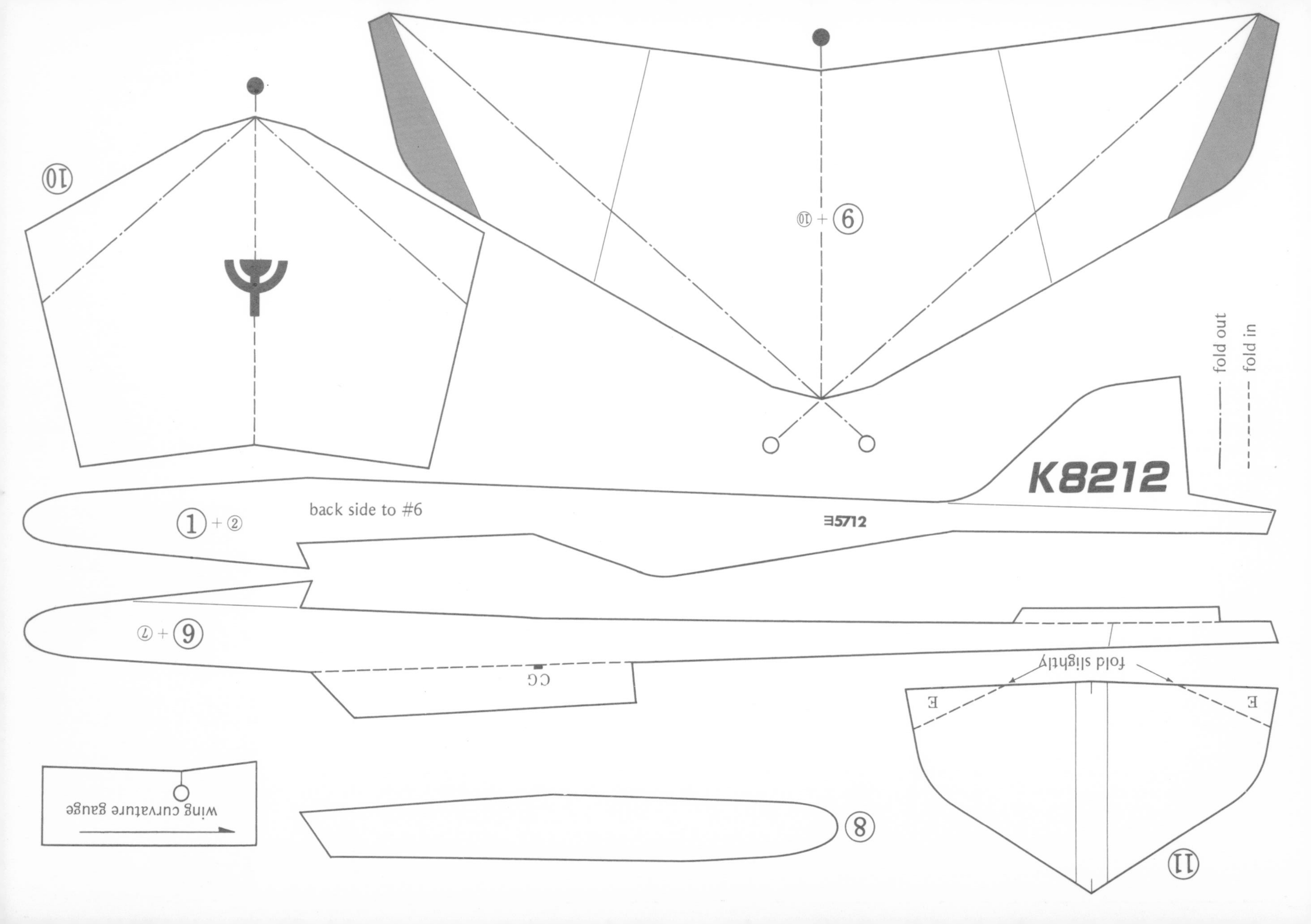
10
9 + 10
fold out
fold in
K8212
1 + 2
back side to #6
6 + 7
CG
fold slightly
E
E
11
wing curvature gauge
8

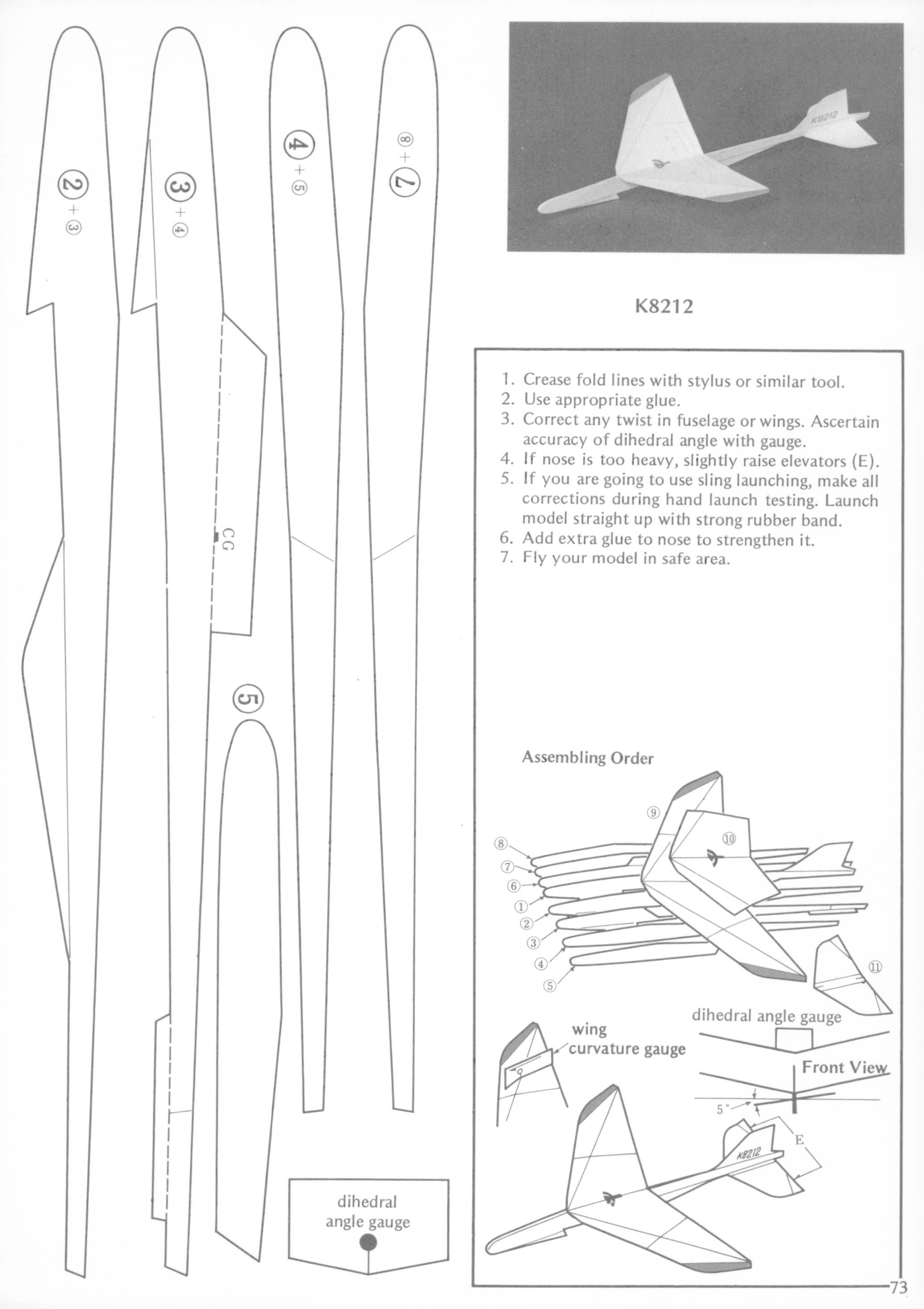
2 + 3
3 + 4
4 + 5
7 + 8
CG
5
dihedral angle gauge
K8212
1. Crease fold lines with stylus or similar tool.
2. Use appropriate glue.
3. Correct any twist in fuselage or wings. Ascertain accuracy of dihedral angle with gauge.
4. If nose is too heavy, slightly raise elevators (E).
5. If you are going to use sling launching, make all corrections during hand launch testing. Launch model straight up with strong rubber band.
6. Add extra glue to nose to strengthen it.
7. Fly your model in safe area.
Assembling Order
9
10
8
7
6
1
2
3
4
5
11
dihedral angle gauge
wing curvature gauge
Front View
5°
E
K8212

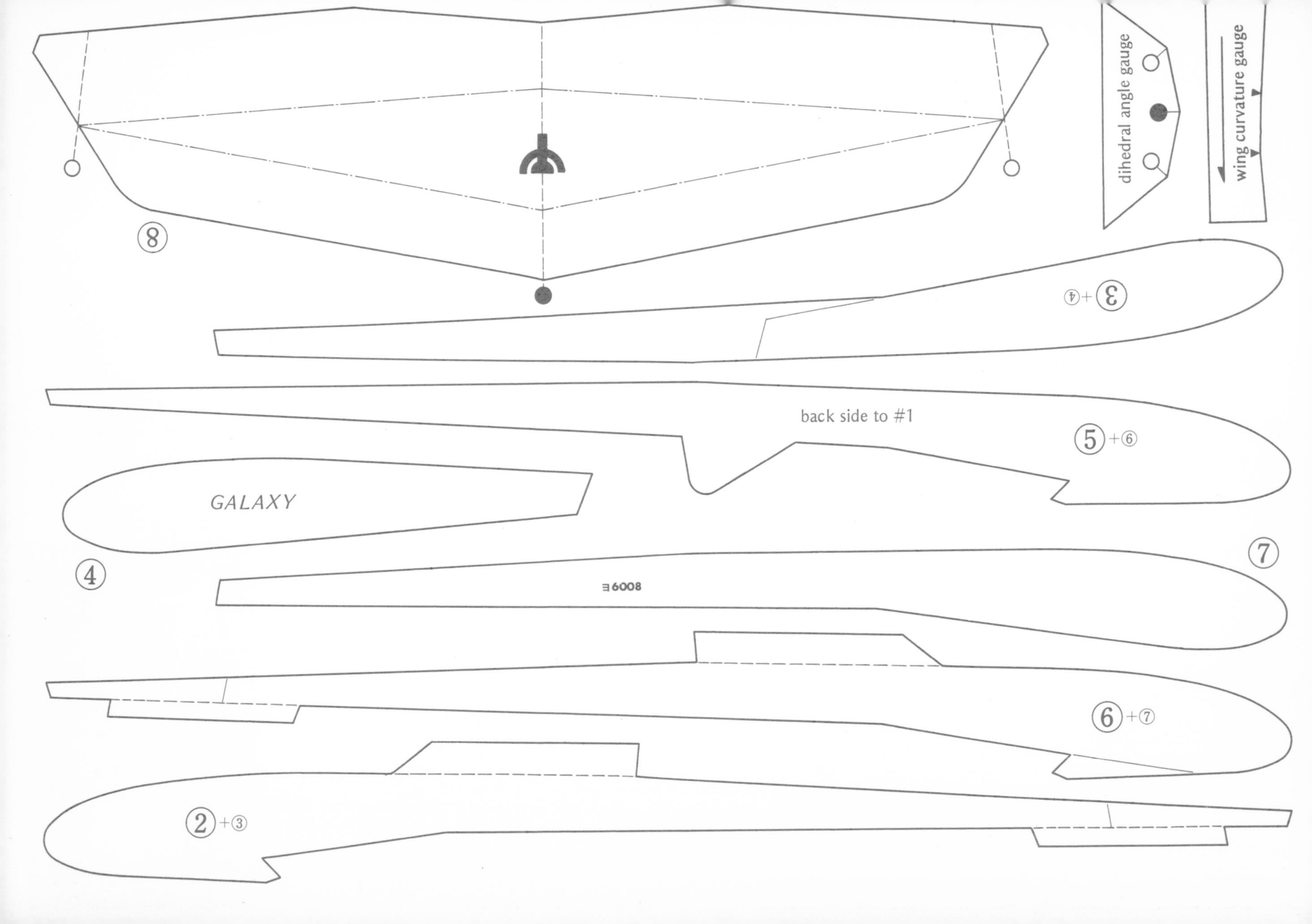
8
dihedral angle gauge
wing curvature gauge
3 + 4
back side to #1
5 + 6
GALAXY
4
7
6 + 7
2 + 3

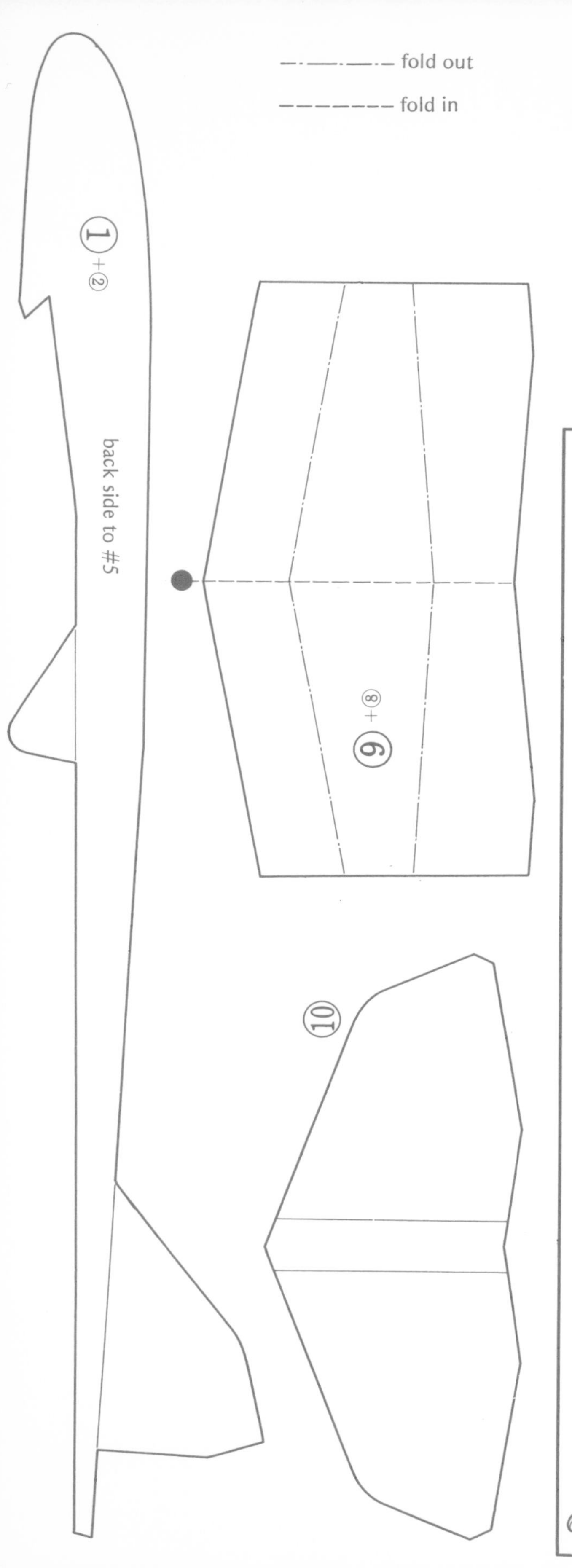

GALAXY

1. Assemble model carefully and patiently. Poor flight is usually due to hasty and incorrect assembly.
2. Crease fold lines with stylus or similar tool.
3. Use appropriate glue.
4. Correct any twist in fuselage or wings. Ascertain accuracy of dihedral angle with gauge.
5. If nose is too heavy, slightly raise elevators (E). If it is too light, slightly lower elevators (E).
6. If you are going to use sling launching, make all corrections during hand launch testing.
7. Fly your model in safe area.

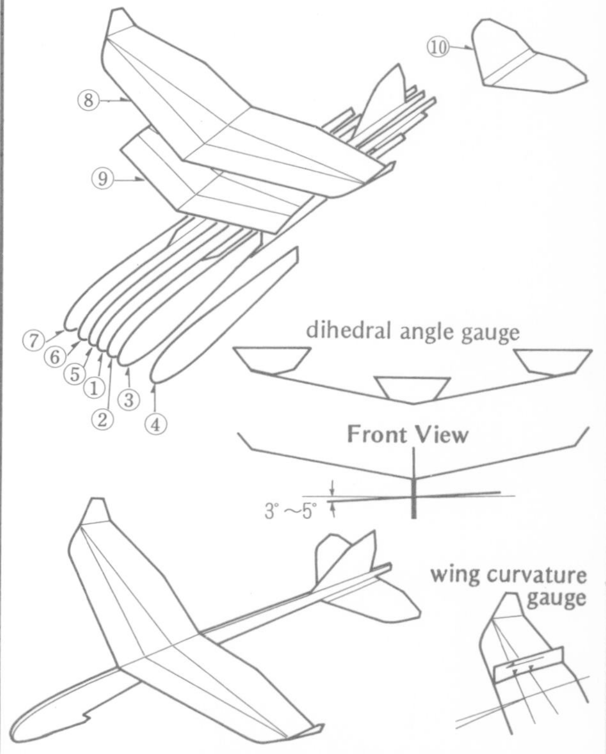

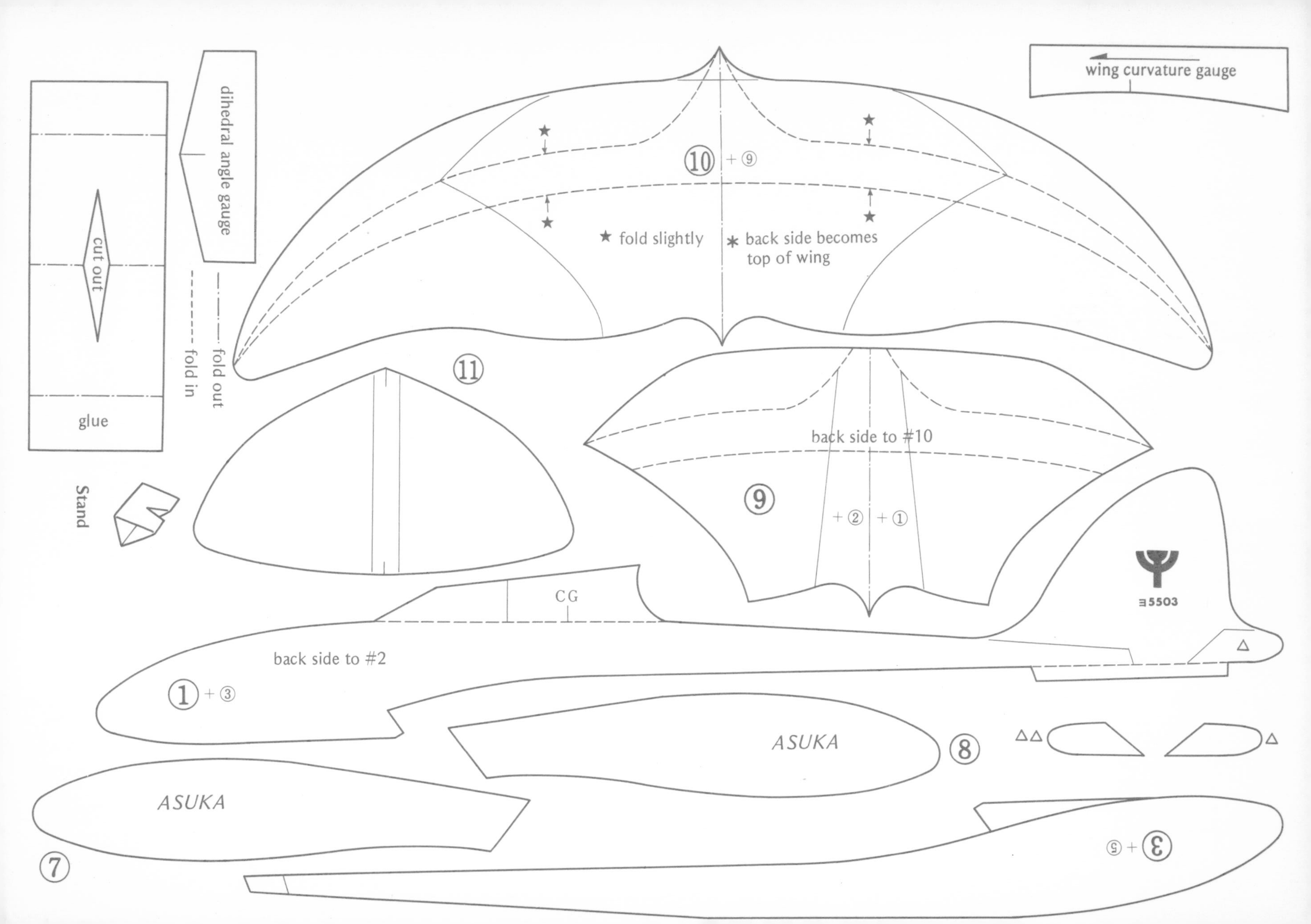
wing curvature gauge
10 + 9
fold slightly
back side becomes top of wing
dihedral angle gauge
cut out
glue
fold out
fold in
Stand
11
back side to #10
9
+ 2 + 1
E5503
CG
back side to #2
1 + 3
ASUKA
8
ASUKA
7
3 + 5